The Deepest Silence
and Other
Essays on Contemporary Spirituality

World Religion Logos

*black-and-white version of the original calligraphy cover artwork
custom hand-painted by Aiko Hayashi,
layout by John Roger Barrie*

The Deepest Silence
and Other
Essays on Contemporary
Spirituality

John Roger Barrie

Sky Parlor Publications™ · Nevada City, California

Library of Congress Control Number: 2024935890

ISBN: 979-8-9866506-8-5 (paperback)
ISBN: 979-8-9866506-9-2 (e-book)

First edition published April 2024

Disclaimer: Mention of various meditation, spiritual, and other practices in this book is intended for educational purposes only and does not constitute professional advice or act as a substitute for seeking expert advice from a qualified medical or other professional. The reader is advised to seek expert personal guidance or medical advice as warranted before undertaking any of these practices.

Sky Parlor Publications™
P.O. Box 252
Nevada City, CA 95959
skyparlorpublications.com

Dedicated to
all sincere spiritual seekers

Also by John Roger Barrie

-*Dialogues With the Lord of Time*
A Novel of Spiritual Awakening

-*First Awakening: A Spiritual Memoir*
Adapted from *Dialogues With the Lord of Time*

Contents

Bonus Writings

Preface

In this collection of writings, I have assembled four previously published articles; three previously unpublished essays; one unpublished parable; and 36 posts I had formerly published on my website, *Explorations in Contemporary Spirituality*, from October 2021 through February 2024. In addition, I've included excerpts from another 13 past website postings and five previously unpublished writings and lectures. As might be expected in such a wide-ranging collection, ideas are sometimes repeated in different essays.

Major themes near and dear to me are found throughout these pages: Prioritize spiritual values and goals above all else. Experiential knowledge of spirituality gained through personal practice is of far greater value than book learning. Be wary of and avoid fraudulent, so-called spiritual teachers.

I have made revisions throughout and minor corrections as warranted. I've expanded the contents of many writings. Where not otherwise credited, I have rendered my own composite versions of translated scriptures and texts. Whenever "he" or "she," "him" or "her," "his" or "hers," or "himself" or "herself" are used as nonspecific pronouns, this usage is intended in a gender-neutral sense.

My hope is that you, dear reader, will find these explorations beneficial in your own spiritual pursuits.

John Roger Barrie
Nevada City, California
April 17, 2024

Acknowledgements

I extend my heartfelt gratitude to the following individuals: pastor and scholar Elizabeth Krajewski, Ph.D., for her extremely helpful manuscript review and comments; editor Rob Bignell, for his top-notch, eagle-eye editing; attorney Jonathan Kirsch, Esq., for his valuable, incisive legal observations; *Parabola* magazine editor and publisher Jeff Zaleski, for believing in and publishing three of these essays; and especially my wife Deborah Griffiths, for her unfailing support while I assembled and prepared this collection of writings for publication.   –JRB

The Deepest Silence

Originally published in *Parabola* magazine
Volume 33, No. 1, "Silence," Spring 2008

THE ELOQUENCE OF THE DEEPEST SILENCE echoes from the eternal. Originating there and reverberating through the ripples of time and space, it bursts forth in shimmering waves, forming light and color, shadow and dimension. But it remains unchanged. Never affected by the slightest permutation of outer phenomena, silence interweaves the temporal but is forever untouched by it.

Ever abiding within and without, overlaid with the mutable patchwork garment we know as this visible universe, silence forms the warp and woof of all things seen and unseen. Yet at any instant it is immanent and accessible. To the mystic, silence is the ground, the core of reality. All else relates to and emanates from it.

The deeper elements in all religions point to this silence. It is God, it is Buddha, it is Allah. But, to paraphrase Lao Tzu,[1] to name it is to elude its essence. It can only be experienced. The sixteenth-century Muslim-born saint Kabir wittily observed, "I laugh when I hear

1

that the fish in the water is thirsty."[2] This paradox, which asserts that we are forever surrounded by silence yet all the while occluded to its existence, forms the key dilemma in spirituality. How can we *not* experience that which always envelops and permeates us? Merely affirming its existence will not garner for us its experiential realization. It is spiritual practice that provides us with the means to fine tune our faculties so we can perceive silence for ourselves. Such practice enables us, over time, to experience a blistering, conscious realization of this silence that suffuses the nucleus of our being.

By embarking on the spiritual path, an aspirant attempts to encounter silence firsthand. This is the quintessential journey in life— our inner pilgrimage. We return to a source long ago forgotten but often glimpsed at moments unawares. Recapturing that which flitters on the periphery of awareness is the goal of the mystic. Firmly abiding in the thundering silence that invisibly drenches us is the teleological aim of life, according to philosopher Gerald Heard (1889–1971).[3] The mystic consciously dives into this silence, at first unfelt. With repeated practice, it becomes a living, palpable Presence filled with immeasurable vitality and boundless, nondual continuity. But what causes this gradual revelation?

First, we need to discover why we do not experience silence. The simplest answer is that we are habituated to noise. We are addicted to novelty, to sensation, to ourselves. Fuss and commotion, mental chatter, and outer stimulation occupy our minds from dawn to dusk. The twentieth-century Zen master Nan-in once poured a cup of tea for a haughty professor until it overflowed.[4] He thus taught him that to learn Zen, he must first empty his mind, which was overflowing with ideas and opinions. But there is often no room for such emptiness in our lives. When one is clattering away on a keyboard and staring into a cellphone multiple hours every day, the capacious pockets of silence are kept well at bay. We thereby deafen ourselves to the underlying silence we would otherwise clearly hear.

By intentionally quieting our restless minds and calling a temporary halt to the random noise—inner and outer—to which we are subjected, we create an environment conducive to the manifestation of silence. Welling up from within, this silence subtly engulfs us, drowning out all the noise of existence. The Jewish mystics refer to

God as *ayin*, nothingness. When we quell the somethingness of our lives, this nothingness emerges. But as long as we dwell in the realm of substance, this emptiness remains elusive.

When constantly engaged at the forefront of our minds, our awareness restlessly flutters from thought to thought, sensation to sensation, thus pushing out silence. The effort—*tapas*—required to break through the surface waves of the mind forges an inward path to the deeper levels of silence. When deliberately sustained via committed, ongoing spiritual practice, this inner drilling displaces the obfuscatory debris that clutters our mind with a matrix of noise. When all mental ruminations are at last exhausted, genuine silence emerges.

There are many different means to contact this silence. The devotee stirs up, then propels affective emotions toward it, transcending their self en route. The intellectual seeker discerns silence from noise, then expels the latter from their mental field. The contemplative eradicates all thought and invites silence to fill the ensuing void. The active aspirant—the busy householder—infuses their actions with a selfless intent that serendipitously chisels through the boundaries of their ego. All four types of practitioners eventually lose themselves in a borderless existence. All effectively dispatch wandering thoughts and narcissistic mentations into a cauldron of deep tranquility, which is the fruit of ripening silence. As the Chinese sage further counsels, "Become empty of yourself and realize inner silence."[5]

But many prefer the comfort of noise, the bustling crowds, the constant engaging of new thoughts and interesting repartee. To embrace silence means splicing off a certain arena of the familiar and venturing into heretofore uncharted territories. While one may fruitfully participate in communal spiritual activities, typically the deeper stages of this voyage are undertaken by oneself. This journey is, as Plotinus maintains, "The flight of the alone to the Alone."[6] To keep the mind occupied with external concerns is to point our inner compass in an outward direction. This is the subtlest trap to which the feeble mind continually succumbs. To interact constantly with the objects of the senses is to eclipse entirely the realm of silence, which is first experienced within. When repeatedly accessed, the decibel level of true silence deafens the resolute mystic.

Ever elusive yet all pervading, silence is known by those who take the leap. The adventuresome hiker seeks areas untrampled by the masses. The successful inner voyager treks to the precipice. Then, having encountered the Unknowable, they brazenly discard map and compass and boldly plunge into the abyss. The yearning heart echoes the cry that seized the Psalmist, "Be still and know that I am God."[7] The knowing mystic, seized with a searing nondual vision, confidently answers back, "Be *silent* and know that you, too, are one with God."

When the Student is Ready

Website post: January 28, 2022

"WHEN THE STUDENT IS READY, THE TEACHER WILL APPEAR." This familiar adage is composed of several key components, which we will analyze in the context of spiritual realization. First, what is a "student"? A person who aspires to realize their full spiritual potential. What is this potential? Ideally, nothing short of full-blown enlightenment. And so, a student is a spiritual aspirant who follows a spiritual path that will unfold the highest realization attainable according to the path they are following.

In the language of Catholic mysticism, this rare state of realization is known as Transforming Union or Spiritual Marriage. In Sufism, it is called *fanā al-fanā* or *baqā*. In Hinduism, it is referred to as *jivanmukta* or *kaivalya* or *turiyatita*. In Theravada Buddhism, it is called *nirvāṇa*. In the Tibetan Buddhist tradition of Dzogchen, it is known as *rigpa*. These advanced states refer to a permanent condition of enlightenment wherein the aspirant's realization is so deeply ingrained that they are inwardly transformed and their illumination remains unchanged no matter what they do.

Ah, but how many students truly focus on the ultimate goal? How many settle for a lesser goal? A person may be content with a sort of comfort religion, whereby their progress comes to a grinding halt at a certain stage.

This leads us to the next component: What is meant by "ready"? Ready simply means being receptive to learn what it takes to advance to the stage of spirituality where the student has set their sights.

Next, what is a "teacher"? The teacher is anything that can lead the student to their goal. Traditionally, a teacher is a person who establishes a deep inner connection with the student and helps them unfold their spiritual essence. The teacher and student usually share a strong karmic bond. But sometimes a teacher is not human. Let's say we aspire to master the virtue of patience. Then our teacher is *every circumstance in life* that presents itself. Each situation we encounter contains a moment that provides an opportunity for us either to advance toward our goal of mastery, or, if ignored, to complacently remain where we are.

A teacher can be a scriptural verse that helps us remain calm and collected amid all the deadlines and obligations we face in our daily rush-rush lives. The teacher also can appear as a dream. A pet can be a teacher. A dramatic sunset can teach. There are no limits to our spiritual teachers. All depends on the student's receptivity.

Finally, what is meant by "appear"? The answer presupposes one key element in the student—*aspiration*. The student must keenly want to attain their spiritual goal. This passionate desire will fuel their journey. The teacher often appears in the midst of the student's fervent attempts to progress; this is more or less a spiritual law. A person can have several spiritual teachers along the way, although usually only one has a primary role. These outer teachers all help to awaken the student's inner teacher. When a dedicated student seriously pursues one of the deeper inner paths to spiritual realization, which they must want more than anything in life, a teacher or teachers will mysteriously appear to help catapult them to the next stage.

We've now reviewed all the components of this wise adage. *When the student is ready, the teacher will appear.* If the student's intentions are focused and noncompromising, they will attain their goal.

Attainment or Unfoldment?
Website post: June 28, 2022

AND SO, THE QUESTION IS RAISED: When undertaking spiritual pursuits, are we attaining something we don't have, or are we unfolding something we already possess? Well, that depends ...

From the perspective of one's ego, we *attain* enlightenment, which we now lack. We strive with all our might and put forth determined efforts to realize our goal. We work to subjugate our at-times unruly ego and make similar attempts to evolve on our spiritual path.

But from another perspective, our innermost essence—our soul or spiritual self (or if Buddhist, our core is considered "emptiness")—is always present, always luminous, but simply concealed, much in the same way when clouds cover the sun. In this sense, spiritual progress consists of *unfolding* this essence by figuratively removing these clouds.

So, which perspective is correct? In reality, both are equally valid. Here's why.

We begin our spiritual journey with our ego, and we end it without our ego. As we progress along the continuum of enlightenment, our ego wanes as our spiritual essence increases. And so there is a dual movement. First, the ego must do all it can to subjugate its own existence, because enhancing the ego is inimical to our spiritual unfoldment. Second, through our diligent pursuit of our spiritual goal, our ego becomes displaced. This very act creates a vacuum, and our spiritual essence fills the resultant void.

The German Dominican priest Johannes Tauler (1300–1361) writes of this transformation from ego to egolessness:

> Everything depends upon this: a fathomless sinking into your own fathomless nothingness. ... The Heavenly Father says, "You shall call me 'My Father' and shall not turn away from me" (Jer 3:19). As if to say, "On and on you must go, deeper and deeper into an unknown and unnamed abyss, nearer and nearer to Me; far above all methods, images, and forms of the mind; your soul stripped naked, your mental faculties lost in Me; and so you must lose yourself, deny yourself, and even unform yourself." Into this lost state of the soul, no ray of light ever shines but one; this light flashes and reveals the all-sufficient being of God—one in essence, one in life, above all. This is not the result of the soul's natural abilities, but of the transformation wrought by the Spirit of God in the created spirit, and the created spirit's bottomless feeling of being lost in God, and its immeasurable disengagement from all that is not God.[8]

From one perspective, there was never a time when we weren't enlightened. But we presently aren't aware of our inherent state of enlightenment, because all the objects in our mind—thoughts, emotions, hopes, memories—obscure this perception. Through spiritual practice, we overcome these obscurations. We remove all the layers that conceal our perception of our intrinsic illumined state. However, it is not our ego that becomes enlightened. Our ego vanishes during the course of our spiritual strivings. What's left is the numinous experience itself—God, the ultimate reality, pure consciousness—minus our ego. The light in our spiritual home is then fully illumined, while its former resident has gone on permanent vacation.

Spiritual Role Models
Website post: August 10, 2022

READING ABOUT AND STUDYING THE LIVES of those who have successfully walked the spiritual path provides helpful examples for us to follow. We can greatly benefit from absorbing what they have learned. In many instances, we can emulate them. These individuals serve as role models, and their lives can inspire us in our own spiritual quest, especially when they hail from the same spiritual tradition we follow.

As opposed to the many me-first and money-first exemplars that dominate the daily headlines, spiritual role models present higher ethical and spiritual standards after which we can pattern ourselves. Instead of witnessing the many ways that humankind expresses hatred toward one another, we can see from the lives of the saints and the saintly how it is possible to love one another. Instead of observing instances of criminal acts against one another, we can see far more inspiring examples of those who selflessly help and give to one another. The spiritual greats show us by their lives what philosopher Gerald Heard called "unlimited liability" in practice. Tibetan

Buddhists call this universal altruistic attitude *bodhichitta*. Over the last century, we've seen Mother Teresa, Dr. Martin Luther King, Jr., the Dalai Lama, and Mahatma Gandhi advance selfless ideals and teachings that serve to raise the bar for us all.

It can also be tremendously supportive for us simply to recall those people who inspire us, especially when dealing with the challenges we face in our lives. For example, when a driver audaciously cuts us off in traffic, we can visualize Jesus in the passenger seat next to us, which would help dictate our response by, ideally, defusing any agitation or animosity that might otherwise envelop us. If we are forced to reprimand an employee at work, think of how Buddha would convey the rebuke. Reading the lives of saints can similarly inspire us to uphold higher ideals and choose the higher road when dealing with irritating individuals and the many vicissitudes of life.

Just as "you are what you eat," so too we become who we imitate. By modeling our lives after the spiritual role models who inspire us, we benefit not only our own spiritual lives but also the lives of others by bettering our interactions with them.

Turning Off the Mind
Website post: August 25, 2023

IN INDIA'S REVERED SCRIPTURE, THE BHAGAVAD GITA, Prince Arjuna complains to Sri Krishna, the celebrated incarnation of God, "O Krishna, the mind is restless, agitated, domineering, and stubborn. I consider it as difficult to control as the wind" (Gita 6:34).

Krishna replies, "Without doubt, the mind is restless and difficult to control, O Arjuna. But, by repeated practice and through detachment, it can be controlled" (Gita 6:35).

The sixth chapter of the Gita is filled with succinct, practical advice on how to turn off the mind and fix it on God. So, why is this important in one's spiritual practice?

In a nutshell, the mind is the fulcrum point, the gateway that leads to one's spiritual self. Typically, one's mind is filled with various desires, emotions, memories of the past, future plans, and lots of restless thoughts. All these things congest the mind. If the mind is emptied of these elements, one's spiritual self (or *atman* in the Gita) can be perceived. This cause-and-effect sequence is confirmed by the great Hindu psychologist Patanjali, author of the classic text, the Yogasūtra, who wrote, "The state of Union occurs when all mental vacillations cease" (Yogasūtra 1:2). Once the sky is free of clouds, one can perceive the sun.

The process of emptying the mind is achieved through concentration and meditation. What is the nature of a concentrated mind? "As the flame of a candle in a windless spot does not flicker, so too does the mind of a Yogi, united with the spiritual Self, remain unmoved" (Gita 6:19).

This state can be attained through repeated practice: "Little by little, a person with firm conviction fixes their mind on the spiritual Self and thinks of nothing else" (Gita 6:25).

This begs the question: Is this state incompatible with functioning in the world? Well, yes and no. A person who sequesters themselves from all distractions when practicing meditation aims to stop their mind entirely. They ordinarily sit in silence during their meditation session, so they cannot and should not be active, but rather motionless. Afterward, when engaging in activity, they carry the imprint of the quietude they attained during practice. This helps to control all the ping-ponging thoughts, emotions, desires, and images that otherwise float through one's mind and sway one to and fro throughout any given day.

Over time, one's spiritual self slowly manifests, like the light of the predawn sun. Concurrently, one's ego diminishes. What is one's ego? Nothing more than a sustained thought. The "I" that we've come to know and love is a particular thought pattern that continually manifests and stubbornly persists. The practice of meditation disrupts all thoughts, including our ego, which is suspended during states of deep concentration. Ultimately, the ego is transcended, as is the mind along with its whirlpool of thoughts, emotions, and mile-a-minute inner chatter. All that remains when one succeeds in turning off the mind is uninterrupted tranquility, unruffled calmness, and unbounded carefree joy.

What Animals Teach Us About Love

Website post: July 11, 2022

THERE IS A DELIGHTFUL NEW BOOK, *Funny Farm: My Unexpected Life with 600 Rescue Animals,* written by Laurie Zaleski, who runs the Funny Farm Animal Rescue, a nonprofit animal sanctuary located in southern New Jersey. The book weaves a remarkable narrative about animals that—get this—get along, and often much better than their human counterparts.

Among the current Funny Farm residents, we learn of a goose named Airplane who follows Emily the emu wherever she goes. Jethro the donkey hangs out with Lorenzo the llama. Cooper the alpaca has found his soulmate in Yogi the steer.

Okay, there are notable exceptions in the wild to the placid utopia found on the Funny Farm. As with humans, not all animals adhere to the Golden Rule, especially when suppertime is calling. Some predatory or territorial animals wouldn't necessarily warm up to a friendly cottontail rabbit seeking cross-species companionship. A ravenously hungry mountain lion couldn't be counted on to lie down in heavenly peace with a docile lamb, per the apocryphal biblical image.

But the larger lesson gleaned from Zaleski's charming book is that many animals can and do get along, and they often behave better than some humans. We can similarly learn from such animal bondings what it might take for us humans to *love one another*. But the first step toward loving one another is respecting one another and being kind and courteous to one another, even if others are vastly different from us. By overlooking these differences, we could well turn our own human funny farm into a more paradisiacal home for us all. Adele the pampered chicken might even cluck her approval of the human species if we did.

True Conversion
Website post: December 24, 2022

"MEN'S COURSES WILL FORESHADOW CERTAIN ENDS, to which, if persevered in, they must lead," said Scrooge. "But if the courses be departed from, the ends will change."

Thus, Ebenezer Scrooge, in Charles Dickens' classic tale of redemption *A Christmas Carol* (1843), put forth the quintessential element of a genuine spiritual conversion experience: one's course of life must change. If so, their former destiny also will change because they are now on a new path.

We can see a similar conversion take place in Saul, who, "breathed out murderous threats against the Lord's disciples" (Acts 9:1), until one fateful day, when he traveled on the road to Damascus. There, "a light from heaven flashed around him" (Acts 9:3). "Then he fell to the ground, and heard a voice say to him:

"Saul, Saul, why do you persecute me?"

"Who art thou, my Lord?"

"I am Jesus, whom you are persecuting" (Acts 9:4–6).

And so, Saul underwent a powerful transformation and became Paul, the staunchest champion of the newfound religion he formerly oppressed.

Other notable spiritual figures underwent transformative conversion experiences. St. Francis (d. 1226) had a vision in which Jesus spoke to him from the crucifix: "Francis, go and rebuild my house." Francis followed his vision. By so doing, he left an indelible mark on Christianity, lasting to this day.

Prince Siddhartha legendarily ventured outside his luxurious palace for the first time at age 29, only to witness an old man, a sick person, a corpse, and an ascetic. Stripped of the protective shelter afforded by his palace, he somberly encountered the all too realistic realities of this world. This stark wakeup call caused him to renounce his princely life and set into motion his subsequent life as the Buddha.

In each instance, Scrooge, Saul, Francis, and Siddhartha were permanently changed. There was no turning back, and they had no regrets about accepting the new life that awaited them. They embraced the *metanoia*, the radical transformation that turned them inside out.

A genuine spiritual conversion totally affects an individual. It's as though they walked from one reality into an entirely different one. The changed person is not the same. The vast majority of people conform with society's norms. Those rare persons who are granted this conversion no longer live and act as we do. They see with new eyes. They fearlessly answer to the demands of their new calling. The critical factor that imbues them with the strength to act on their transformation: *they never compromise.*

"Scrooge was better than his word. He did it all, and infinitely more. ... He became as good a friend, as good a master, and as good a man, as the good old city knew, or any other good old city, town, or borough, in the good old world. ... And it was always said of him, that he knew how to keep Christmas well, if any man alive possessed the knowledge. May that be truly said of us, and all of us!" Dickens wrote.

Those who have undergone a true spiritual conversion inspire us on our own path. These noncompromising spiritual giants and fictional heroes set a benchmark for us to follow. Their lives provide hope and rouse courage as we journey toward our goal. We'll let Dickens have the last word. "And so, as Tiny Tim observed, 'God bless Us, Every One!'"

The Future Is an Illusion
Previously unpublished essay: June 2009

Dear, dear! How queer everything is today! And yesterday things went on just as usual.

—*Alice in Wonderland* by Lewis Carroll

WHEN ALICE PONDERED HER FATE while wading in a pool of tears, she left one very important element out of the equation—tomorrow. What, pray tell, will become of her tomorrow? For that matter, what will become of any of us tomorrow? We can infer that the imminent future will likely unfold according to a fairly predictable trajectory. Unless we travel, begin our weekend, or an emergency arises, tomorrow will be more or less the same as today. But what becomes of us after a thousand, or ten thousand tomorrows? Therein are revealed the consequences of our being subjected to the unalterable progression of time. Time is change, and changeability is woven into the very fabric of time.

17

Alice concludes her existential musings by asking, "Was I the same when I got up this morning? ... But if I'm not the same, the next question is, Who in the world am I? Ah, *that's* the great puzzle!"

Alice's great puzzle constitutes the basic conundrum of life. All aspects of our material and psychological existence are in a state of constant flux. Who we are today is not quite the same as who we were yesterday. Our cells age, our thought patterns vary, and our emotions vacillate. Yet, according to one Eastern philosophy—Vedanta—the most significant component within us remains untouched by change. This is called the *atman*—our true self, our innermost spiritual essence. But, because of our psychological conditioning, we mistakenly identify our self with our body, mind, emotions, and, most absurdly, our possessions. Yet underneath these external elements lies the immutable core of our being. Who we are is not our physical makeup, our personality, or our moods. We are, fundamentally, pure unadulterated consciousness.

Of all earthbound species, seemingly only humans have the most developed capacity for reflection, forethought, and abstract conceptualizations. Only we possess a highly complex nervous system capable of sustaining an acute sense of self-awareness. Only we can experience mystical union, *nirvāṇa*, *samadhi*, and similar states of higher consciousness. And only we can contemplate the meaning of time. But ... what actually is time?

According to lay philosopher William D. Conner (1934–2018), time is a "progression of events ... a comparison of events."[9] By comparing a snapshot taken today with one taken a year ago, the effects of time become evident. We notice change. But as Conner asserts, "There is no time at all in the universe itself. Time resides solely in the mind of the sentient being who observes time phenomena."[10] It is we who interpret the flow of events and divide this flow according to past, present, and future. While this arrangement accommodates social conventions, such as work schedules and the regulation of daily life, it is an inaccurate characterization of time. The measurement of time is a mental construct, an artificial account that is overlaid on to the flow of events "to organize sensory stimuli coming to us,"[11] as psychologist Charles T. Tart (b. 1937) writes.

When scientists at the Illinois-based Fermilab discovered in 2006 that a certain subatomic particle oscillates between matter and antimatter states at three trillion times per *second,* they unwittingly confirmed the ancient Hindu theory of a vibrating universe. The Vedic seers maintained that the fundamental constituent of the universe is vibration, which they perceived aurally. They discerned this vibration through direct revelation and termed it "Om." Om is said to be the universal drone or *pranava*—the whirring reverberatory hum that forms the underlying matrix of physical existence. "In reality, Om is the entire universe,"[12] the *rishis* or seers of old declared. The late Rabbi David Cooper (1939–2020) noted that it took a primordial spark or "nudge" to set in motion this whole cosmic process and continually sustain it from moment to moment. "If the nudge were withdrawn even one of the [three] trillion times, it would all collapse. Creation would disappear,"[13] he maintained.

The universe is thus composed of a series of pulsations occurring so rapidly that they seem to form solidity and dimension. But if the plug were pulled, *poof!* Everything would vanish. By way of analogy, a digital television signal is typically transmitted at 30 frames per second. If one could slow down the rate of oscillation, a flicker is revealed. It is our inability to perceive the flicker that lends substance to the so-called objective reality we perceive, because the universe's rapid rate of vacillation obscures the underlying flux. But the flicker is the primary underlying fact of material existence, whether it vibrates at 30 or three trillion times per second. And so, we humans wobble through our existential "reality," which appears, disappears, then conveniently reconstructs itself from nanosecond to nanosecond.

The field of quantum mechanics holds that an observer is an intimate part of what they observe. It is impossible to separate the perception of reality from the perceiver; both are part of a single process. In Vedic philosophy, the three components of perception—observer, observed, and the process of observation—are known as the *triputi.* However, the foundational inner spiritual reality—the *atman,* one's spiritual self—cannot be objectified; it exists beyond this circuitous threefold process. Hence, objective reality can be seen as illusory because perception is dependent upon an observer who is "imposing a conceptual framework" (Dr. Tart)[14] on what is perceived, thus distorting it. This conceptual framework consists of human in-terpretations of data according to certain criteria (e.g., language, definitions, classifications), which are relative, not absolute. Such criteria are based on intellectual categorizations, social agreements, and utilitarian conveniences. This framework assumes the existence of a three-dimensional universe that is bound by physical laws and held together by the glue of time. But as physicist Paul Davies (b. 1946) cautions, "Fundamental things like duration, length, past, present and future can no longer be regarded as a dependable frame-work within which to live our lives."[15]

So what is it we actually perceive? What are these pulsations that flicker on and off and appear oh so real? Einstein taught us that mat-ter is condensed energy. Energy is subject to Newton's law of recip-rocal actions, which is roughly equivalent to the Vedic theory of karma. The theory of karma posits that every action produces a re-action; every cause produces an effect. Proponents of the theory of karma believe it provides plausible explanations for many phenom-ena, both universal and personal. St. Paul writes of a parallel concept that applies to our lives in the context of Christianity, "Whatever you sow, that you will reap" (Gal. 6:7).

In Vedanta, the Chandogya Upanishad asserts, "In the beginning (before creation), there was Being alone, one only, without a second. That Being willed, 'May I become many, may I grow forth' " (VI.2.2–3).[16] Thus propelled by the divine spark—Rabbi Cooper's nudge—the evolution of the universe began according to Hinduism. Conscious-ness then expanded (*pravritti*) and assumed various names and forms. From the subtle to the gross, from mind to matter, we can witness the multiplicity of creation. What pushes the universe along on its jour-ney is the snowball-like, cause-and-effect momentum of karma.

And so, karma can be viewed as the force that forms and re-forms matter anew each second. What we perceive at any given mo-ment is a microscopic slice of the karmic pie. The continuum of karma is like an assembly line. Packets of karma await the split sec-ond when it's their turn to assemble themselves and appear in the visible universe. Once they manifest for their moment in the lime-light, they again disassemble. Those packets awaiting manifestation we term the future; those already manifest we term the past. This karmic continuum continues unabated for countless eons until the universal Being of Upanishadic lore withdraws the creation back unto itself, just "as a spider sends forth then withdraws its own web" (Mundaka Upanishad 1.1.7). The journey of evolution thus involves the primal Being eventually retracting (*nivritti*) and shedding its myriad names and forms—its coat of many colors—in order to reunite with itself in singularity.

The configurations of karma we encounter on a daily basis—the various situations in our lives—are simply dense *representations* of karma in action. The physical universe is a medium for playing out the continual unfolding of karma. Our earthly realm is a karmic platform wherein desires and emotions—likes and dislikes, attachments and aversions—are expressed, and, by undertaking spiritual practices, transcended. The body and mind serve as the gross loci through which karma is acted out. "All the world's a stage ..." The problem lies in our entrenched belief that the universe and we are real. We take all this too seriously. Like watching an absorbing movie, we get caught up in the drama. We forget who we really are—a spiritual being, the *atman*, the detached witness of the movie—and not the participant. The participant—composed of packets of karma that have no real existence—is a projected image, a transitory vehicle through which karma is enacted.

To spiritually illumined souls, time does not exist. These enlightened beings actually *experience* each object they encounter as impermanent. Through their enlightened eyes, they can actually see each thing re-creating itself from moment to moment, then dissolving just as rapidly. They perceive the underlying flicker. Such souls have succeeded in bracketing off their consciousness from all involvement with change, with time. Instead of being caught in the continuum of linear time and imprisoned by the suffocating confines of humans' persistent intellectual categorization of all things, they are immersed in an eternal present moment so intense that it completely overshadows the illusory, seemingly solid reality that impinges at every turn. (This eternal present moment is altogether different from the ordinary present tense we normally experience; it has no beginning and no end—it transcends all flux and resides beyond the dimensions of space and time.)

These illumined souls witness their apparition-like body–mind mechanism going through its karmic motions. But they are not inwardly involved with this temporal mirage. By identifying their true self with pure consciousness, which forever stands apart from time, they are able to surf atop Infinity.

By undergoing spiritual practices, we, too, can experience firsthand this heightened state. The promise of all experiential mystical paths is not merely imbuing one with an intellectual understanding of their abstract principles, but experientially conferring on the dedicated aspirant a scintillating realization of their deepest truths. When we reach this state, we are infused with a perspective so vast that, as philosopher Gerald Heard (1889–1971) writes, we "are able to reinterpret correctly the experience which we call Time and, doing so, we see Reality no longer distorted, but as it is."[17]

Once liberated from the grip of time, we are better able to address the quandary posed by Alice's great puzzle. *"Who in the world am I?"* "I" am infinite consciousness, unbounded by matter, unfettered by the names and forms that swirl through the cosmos, and ever free from the implacable constraints of time.

[April 2025 update: "The Future Is an Illusion" was selected for publication in the Spring 2025 issue of *Parabola* magazine, Volume 50, No. 1, "The Mystery of Time," which was *Parabola's* last issue.]

Narendra and Martin:
We Share Your Dreams
Website post: January 14, 2023

TODAY IS THE ANNUAL COMMEMORATION (*Jayanti*) of Narendra Nath Datta's birth. Narendra, better known as Swami Vivekananda (1863–1902), singlehandedly put Hinduism on the map in America. Vivekananda preached a universal, interfaith message, upholding respect for all peoples and religions. The paradigm-shifting swami first widely declared his message during the World's Parliament of Religions, which convened in September 1893 in Chicago. When he uttered his opening words, "Sisters and brothers of America," the audience gave him a standing ovation for two minutes.

On Monday, we celebrate the national holiday honoring twentieth-century American martyr Dr. Martin Luther King, Jr. (1929–1968). He delivered his iconic "I Have a Dream" speech at the pivotal March On Washington demonstration in 1963. But Dr. King's sublime oration almost didn't come about. He was reading a prepared text and was about to sit down, when renowned Gospel singer Mahalia Jackson, who was seated to his left, shouted to him, "Tell them about the dream, Martin!" This caught his attention. Jackson again shouted, "Tell 'em about the dream!" Dr. King set aside his prewritten remarks and, over the next 17 minutes, walked into history with his indelible, heart-stirring words.

We'll review significant passages from each speech, given nearly 70 years apart. First is an excerpt from Swami Vivekananda's World's Parliament of Religions address, delivered on September 11, 1893:

> Sisters and brothers of America, ... Sectarianism, bigotry, and its horrible descendant, fanaticism, have long possessed this beautiful earth. They have filled the earth with violence, drenched it often and often with human blood, destroyed civilization and sent whole nations to despair. Had it not been for these horrible demons, human society would be far more advanced than it is now. But their time is come; and I fervently hope that the bell that tolled this morning in honor of this convention may be the death-knell of all fanaticism, of all persecutions with the sword or with the pen, and of all uncharitable feelings between persons wending their way to the same goal.

Next is the well-known, impassioned passage from Dr. Martin Luther King, Jr.'s "I Have A Dream" speech, given on August 28, 1963:

> I have a dream that one day this nation will rise up and live out the true meaning of its creed: We hold these truths to be self-evident, that all men are created equal. ... And when this happens, and when we allow freedom ring, when we let it ring from every village and every hamlet, from every state and every city, we will be able to speed up that day when all of God's children, Black men and white men, Jews and Gentiles, Protestants and Catholics, will be able to join hands and sing in the words of the old Negro spiritual: "Free at last. Free at last. Thank God almighty, we are free at last."

Narendra and Martin—two spiritual siblings in God, preaching universal equality and humankind's urgent need to love one another.

The Not So Gentle Jesus
Website post: October 9, 2022

WHILE WE READ THE MANY NEW TESTAMENT ACCOUNTS that bolster the mild-mannered image of Jesus as portrayed in Charles Wesley's famous hymn, *Gentle Jesus, Meek and Mild*, there is another side of Jesus we cannot ignore. "Do you think I have come to bring peace on earth? No, I tell you, but rather division," he declared (Luke 12:51). Further, "I have come to ignite a fire on the earth, and how I wish it were already kindled!" (Luke 12:49).

Jesus indeed ignited that fire. During the past two millennia, he has emerged as arguably the most influential person in the Western world, either directly or indirectly. So, what division did Jesus bring about? What fire did he kindle?

In this essay, we will neither address Jesus' messianic assertions (i.e., that he was the Jewish *mashiach*, though his was a spiritual and not a secular kingdom) nor his apocalyptic predictions (e.g., "Nation will rise up against nation, and kingdom against kingdom" Matt. 24:7). Instead, we will delve into one of Jesus' primary missions of injecting spirituality back into religion, much as Moses had done centuries earlier. Jesus shook up the religious establishment, and he steadfastly refused to compromise his ideals. He took to task the religious leaders of his time in no uncertain terms.

Jesus never minced words when using terms such as "blind guides," "hypocrites," "snakes," and "brood of vipers" to describe those he accused of usurping the primacy of God by emphasizing the customs of man. He vividly demonstrated his opposition to the secularization of religion when overturning the moneychangers' tables within the sacred Temple grounds in Jerusalem (Matt. 21:12–13). Jesus was a spiritual reformer, and he radically sought to reintroduce vital spiritual values and practices back into his religion, which he strongly felt it lacked.

What really set off Jesus was what he deemed were the hypocrisies he witnessed by the religious leaders of his day. In Matthew 23, Jesus lets loose in a lengthy tirade composed of seven "woes" directed at those who held religious power. The series of diatribes constitutes Jesus' quintessential invective toward religious hypocrisy. We are fortunate to have this detailed account, because those same principles that applied then have equally applied throughout the subsequent centuries to all those who hold power in any religious tradition, and they most certainly apply now.

Jesus demonstrated singular courage for pointing out, as in the Hans Christian Andersen fairy tale, that in his estimation the religious "emperors" of his day wore no clothes, and this certainly did nothing to endear him to the reigning religious elders. Nowadays, we see factions within Christianity that entirely discount this all-important message. A certain percentage of those who overlook the lessons gleaned from Jesus' teachings on religious hypocrisy are the very ones who personify it. Jesus' uncompromising message applies all the more to so-called Christians who promote gospels of hatred, not love; war, not peace; exclusivity, not inclusiveness; and demonstrate a snobbish holier-than-thou sanctimonious arrogance. Such quote-unquote Christians and Christian churches actually lead people away from God, not to God.

The not so gentle Jesus kindled a fire to burn up all forms of religious hypocrisy and corruption. On the one hand, he created division in order to unfetter his culture from what he regarded as a rigid adherence to religious practices that were void of deeper meaning because he felt they were cut off from the living source of spirituality—God. On the other hand, he sought to instill genuine inner transformation by counseling others to adhere to and embody purely spiritual values. And therein lies the real significance and lesson of Jesus' actions for us today.

Jesus instructed aspirants to practice what they preach and, echoing Moses before him, to "Love the Lord your God with all your heart, and with all your soul, and with all your mind, and with all your strength" (Mark 12:30, based on Deut. 6:5). He enjoined his followers to seek God above all things (Matt. 6:33). He taught a path of limitless, unconditional love toward all others: "Love your neighbor as yourself" (Mark 12:31, based on Lev. 19:18). "Those who have ears, let them hear" (Matt. 11:15). Who is listening?

Two Facets of a Religion

Excerpt from lecture delivered at the Friends of the Spirit
study group in Redding, California: July 24, 1986

The philosopher Gerald Heard likened the contemplative life to that of a pure researcher and the active life to that of an applied researcher.[18] While both aspects are needed for a balanced spiritual life, a person will naturally be drawn to one or the other, based on their temperament. However, there are weaknesses to which both approaches can succumb if one is followed to the exclusion of the other.

A contemplative life with no outer expression can become a self-oriented rather than a God-oriented concern. Thus, the very purpose of such a life is defeated. An active religious life that is devoid of an inner connection with God soon loses the very foundation upon which it must stand.

Without the balancing influence of the other, each approach ceases to be dynamically infused with a panoramic vision of purpose. When one path is followed while excluding the other, it can lead to a partial spirituality. But together, both approaches form an interdependent relationship—each drawing from the other and reciprocating back to the other—as shared components of a single, comprehensive expression of one's spirituality.

What is needed, then, is a decompartmentalization of these two facets that would allow for both to exist simultaneously without conflict or cyclical swings. In this context, the fourteenth-century Flemish Christian mystic John Ruysbroeck (1293–1381) wrote in his *Adornment of the Spiritual Marriage* of "the third way."[19] In this balanced, heightened spiritual state, "God comes to us without ceasing ... and demands of us both action and [mystical] fruition, in such a way that the one never impedes, but always strengthens, the other. And therefore the most inward person lives their life in these two ways: namely, in work and in rest. And in each he is whole and undivided; for he is wholly in God because he rests in [mystical] fruition, and he is wholly in himself because he loves in activity."[20] According to Ruysbroeck, "This is the highest degree of the ... interior life."[21]

Seeing God in All Beings
Website post: April 24, 2022

INDIA'S GREAT SCRIPTURE, THE BHAGAVAD GITA, contains profound lessons for us all. One verse states, "An accomplished yogi sees God in all beings, and all beings in God; that person sees the same God everywhere" (Gita 6:29). The scripture variously explains this key statement.

When we perceive other beings with our present dualistic consciousness, we more often than not don't perceive God in them. Rather, we perceive the various material formations wrought by their karma: their body, their personality, their actions. The Gita points out that all these formations are merely the workings of nature and are not the real person: "It is nature that engages in these acts" (Gita 5:14). So, from this perspective, what we see when we perceive others are the workings of nature and the flutterings of their karma.

Then how can we see beyond others' karma—their outer shell—which can be wondrously virtuous, as in a saint, or profoundly evil, as we often read in the daily news?

The Gita gives instructions on different means to achieve spiritual illumination that vary according to one's temperament. Through *dedicated spiritual practice,* one is able to employ inner knowledge (*jnana* yoga) and perform selfless spiritualized actions (*karma* yoga) to become enlightened. Secondary practices are also mentioned, such as devotion (*bhakti* yoga) and meditation (*dhyāna* yoga, which is technically not the same as the meditation technique outlined in Patanjali's eight-limbed path of yoga). All such practices help to peel away the false layers that cover one's spiritual self.

When stripped of these illusory overlays that comprise one's outer being, all that's left is God. When one attains this elevated state, their inner vantage point changes. The now-illumined soul is capable of seeing "that all activity occurs because of the continual interactions of changing material processes" (Gita 13:30). They can see beyond others' karma and perceive God in them. They are additionally able to see "the same God everywhere." Such a state can be attained in this very life. What are we waiting for?

Have We Been Deluding Ourselves?
Website post: November 5, 2022

WHERE ONE'S SPIRITUAL LIFE IS CONCERNED, aspirants can easily get sidetracked. One of the biggest traps can often be, oddly enough, reading books about spirituality. Or, more precisely, reading pseudo-spiritual books. Pseudo-spiritual books are those that contain oodles of abstract concepts, focus on psychic or unexplained phenomena, or are filled with, for lack of a better word, gobbledygook.

The Zen master Hui-Neng is depicted in one drawing as tearing up the scriptures. This is not due to any particular irreverence or a perverse attitude on his part, but because he realized that no printed word can lead one to spiritual realization. A superficial reading of the scriptures without probing their deeper meaning can lead to stagnation on one's spiritual journey. Worse, a slavish recital of the scriptures without putting into practice their key teachings can cause one to miss their spiritual point entirely.

There are other traps as well. Beliefs form the foundation of religious life. They provide a framework for one's faith. But beliefs can become a rigid, strangulating dogma for some. If a spiritual aspirant becomes beholden to this kind of stilted dogma, it can provide a false sense of assuredness. To think that the smug repetition of dogmatic assertions will lead one to heaven is the surest road to hell. While all aspirants need a basic roadmap to guide them on the path to enlightenment, a shallow parroting of inflexible doctrinal tenets can paralyze one's spiritual growth.

One of the biggest deceptions is the false hope engendered by believing that understanding theories about religion, spirituality, or consciousness will help one to become enlightened. Nothing could be further from the truth. To equate an understanding of theories with spiritual realization is like saying that night is the same as day. One can discuss God *ad infinitum*, but such discussions will never ferry you to God's inner abode.

Spiritual realization is a searing experience that transforms an aspirant's very being. One's ego is dissolved. Their false identity collapses. All points on their inner compass implode. "We" do not survive spiritual enlightenment. The "I" that we've come to know and identify with is extinguished when we are spiritually illumined. "Extinguish" is the meaning of the word *nirvāṇa*. The resultant state can neither be imagined nor described. Only experienced.

Aspirants can spend their entire spiritual life unmindfully adhering to beliefs, memorizing cumbersome dogma, and entertaining abstract theories. By so doing, they will have wasted their time, for they are not transforming themselves. They should not allow themselves to be thus deluded.

On a more personal level, the tried-and-true way to spiritual enlightenment is through sincere and dedicated practice, regardless of our path. A fervent resolve takes hold of our inner being and turns us inside out. Allow for this to happen. Ignore what the masses think and do, and pay no attention to the marketing purveyors who promote the latest teacher *du jour* or the next big-deal faddish book. "Only one thing is needful" (Luke 10:42) as Jesus reminds us. That one thing is our total, undivided, and passionate devotion to our spiritual goal. All else is a distraction. To think otherwise is to be misled. Missing the opportunity to evolve spiritually in this life is the ultimate means by which we delude ourselves.

When Religion Does More Harm Than Good

Website post: January 27, 2024 (revised March-April 2024)

A NEW POLL REVEALS that the religious unaffiliated, the "Nones," now constitute the majority of all such groups in America, topping even established religions. The Jan. 24, 2024, NPR article, *Religious 'Nones' are now the largest single group in the U.S.*, details this finding. In 2007, the number of "Nones" stood at 16%. The new statistics, compiled during 2023, show this figure has dramatically increased to a whopping 28%. Nearly half (43%) of the "Nones" say that "religion does more harm than good"[22] in contemporary American society.

If this is the case, then organized religion is in a sorry state. But we've known this for a long time. Conventional religion often does not fill peoples' lives with meaning, relevance, or provide them with purposeful spiritual goals, ironic as this may seem. Why is this?

The reason, from my perspective, is because most Western religions do not readily offer *experiential* means to realize God. The largest slice of the American religious pie consists of Christians—mainly

Protestants and Catholics. Attending a one-hour religious service once a week doth not transform lives. Reciting a codified dogma year after year can become an unmindful parroting of lifeless words when it lacks the mystical element. Participating in religious social functions is often nothing more than attending a coffee klatch at church instead of the workplace. Religion especially turns ugly when used as a forum to propagate political beliefs or, even more chillingly, to justify bigotry, racially motivated violence, or war.

By the same token, many churchgoers do find meaning and purpose in their lives. The rousing Black denominations get it right when pouring out their hearts in devotional outcries during services. Cultivating and expressing heartfelt devotion is an expedient path to God, and a devout practitioner can, by virtue of their single-minded devotion, transcend any bureaucratic or theological limitations found within their church. Many Orthodox Christians follow inner practices aimed at establishing deep communion with God. Catholicism has its own rich history of mystical practices, if one takes the time to find them.

But dogmatic religion, socializing religion, and political religion are not fulfilling the true mission of genuine religion. The word "religion" is derived from the Latin *religāre*, which means "to bind." The true purpose of religion is to bind one's soul back to God. This is accomplished by routinely undertaking practices, such as meditation, prayer, spiritualized actions, devotion, and selfless service, all of which help to change one's nature and unfold their spiritual core.

Other than stating that religion "encourages superstition and causes division," the new poll does not define *why* the "Nones" believe religion does more harm than good. Is it due to social policy stances? Or because of creationism theory? Or a predominantly male clergy? This is an oversight of the polling organization, Pew Research Center, which failed to drill deep in order to ascertain this information.

So, let's further examine these polling terms. "Superstition" is a relative word, subject to interpretation. One person's superstition is another's *Weltanschauung*. "Causes division"—the pollsters neglected to define this. But we all know what happens when a group of dogmatic-minded individuals attempts to impose their myopic, often hate-filled fanatical views on others—this indeed creates division.

But I'll offer some additional reasons. From Protestantism has emerged the unctuous, and odious, self-inflated preacher type—often power-hungry authoritarian ministers who lord over others. These toxic pastors are plagued by superiority complexes or at the very least are incorrigibly arrogant and shamelessly self-righteous. Next are the fraudulent faith healers, who act more like carnival barkers than true servants of God. And, equally offensive—the often shady, corrupt televangelists who, like the fake healers, are frequently only in it for the money. If Dante's vision of Hell were a reality, I can't help but wonder if these greedy charlatans are unsuspectingly using the ill-gotten gains they've pilfered from their gullible flocks to purchase for themselves a one-way ticket to the ninth circle of Hell, where Lucifer himself is said to dwell. You can conduct an internet search to discover their net worth, which often rivals sports players, and you can view their mega-mansions in all their sprawling extravagant glory. We've witnessed one scandal after another among the televangelists.

Within Catholicism, we've witnessed the Church's deplorable historical atrocities alongside its staggering, excessive cumulative wealth, which is ostentatiously displayed while many of its followers live in abject poverty. The Catholic Church has at times participated in the very worst of sinful acts—the bloodbaths of the Crusades, the barbaric carnages of the Inquisition, the Conquistadorian genocides, the selling of papal indulgences, simony, and more recently, the abysmally horrific child sexual-abuse scandals along with their indefensible cover-ups, which are inexcusably heinous and should see the criminal perpetrators and their accomplices immediately defrocked and fully prosecuted.

Now, I was raised Catholic; I follow certain Catholic observances, and I am an advocate and practitioner of Catholic mysticism, which is a centuries-old authentic, vibrant spiritual tradition. I am grateful that the Church hosts these practices and upholds this heritage. I'm equally grateful that the vast majority of priests are reputable. But these degenerate aspects play no part in my Catholicism. I am among those Catholics and non-Catholics alike who wholly denounce and categorically repudiate these appalling, malignant elements, which have no place in any religion.

I believe Jesus would be sorely ashamed of, staunchly condemn, and vigorously rebuke the sanctioning of such chicanery as papal indulgences—just the sort of corruption he railed against—and the torturous killings of the Inquisition—the complete antithesis of the universal love and tolerance he advocated. I believe he would especially revile the many exemplars of moral turpitude that have infested His church in the form of priests and clergy who are supposed to represent him yet who prey on children for their own wanton lascivious gratification.

As for amassing disproportionate wealth, Jesus clearly instructed, "You still lack one thing. Sell everything you own and distribute the proceeds to the poor, and you will have treasure in heaven ..." (Luke 18:22). On a similar note, the very epitome of corruption is the so-called Prosperity Gospel, wherein debased preachers hold that if one believes in Jesus, they'll be showered with money, money, money, oh, and lots of possessions to boot. This is a singularly vile distortion of everything for which Jesus stood. These false teachers and wolves in sheep's clothing personify everything unethical, dishonest, and unscrupulous that has oozed its way into Christianity. These deceitful con artists, perpetuating the adoration of money and possessions, are simply using Jesus as a means to increase their own wealth. They have nothing to do with the true gospel of Jesus. This Prosperity Gospel is just as abhorrent as the crooked televangelists' many dumbfoundingly horrendous and ethically bankrupt transgressions. Jesus amply demonstrated his disdain for double-dealing hypocrisy. He would no doubt vehemently denounce and censure these out-and-out charlatans and parasitic, self-serving frauds.

Perhaps Jesus would found a new church, without all these corruptions (isn't this what St. Francis did?), and with a system of checks and balances to maintain integrity and transparency, and with an instantly enforceable zero-tolerance policy. And maybe he would decentralize it more, as in Orthodox Christianity, so there wouldn't be an elite coterie of authoritarian bureaucrats and faceless administrators who often run the show. And perhaps he might minimally structuralize it so it would be something akin to a community network, similar to the Early Church, of study and practice groups whose aims are both cultivating and spreading universal love outside of a dogmatic theological context and fostering experiential spiritual realization without all the red tape.

Of course, my criticism focuses on the most visible, most reprehensible, and most condemnatory and contemptible acts within both Catholicism and Protestantism: widespread child sexual abuse among a shocking 1.5% to 5% of the worldwide Catholic priesthood between 1959 and 2009;[23] an estimated 260 child sexual-abuse claims per year among Protestant denominations in the U.S. over a 20-year period;[24] and let's not forget the 2019 sex-abuse scandal that rocked the Southern Baptist Convention.[25] One finding indicates sexual-abuse statistics are highest among Protestant churches.[26] All such abusers should immediately be fired and prosecuted to the fullest extent of the law. Even one incident is one incident too many.

Okay, we've recounted scandals, slaughters, money-grubbing shysterism, and the often hierarchical, out-of-touch church authorities, all of which are off-putting to many. What of the insidious religious cults, characteristically headed by abusive, messianic, Svengali-like despots? We have seen the truly deranged and dangerous. Peoples Temple, the Branch Davidians, and Heaven's Gate are among the most egregious recent historical examples, but a slew of such groups always crops up. Along with the unfortunate victims, cults are fueled both by weak-willed individuals who inscrutably allow the sociopathic, manipulating leaders to control their lives, and by brainwashed accomplices who enable these unhinged maniacs. The "Nones" witness this madness. Unquestionably, "religion does more harm than good" in such instances.

Also, when religion is used in the name of war or as a political mouthpiece, it ceases being a religion. Period. Neither is religion a form of entertainment, although it's sometimes hard to tell the difference.

It doesn't take a rocket scientist to understand how these issues may constitute some of the reasons why the "Nones" are amassing such huge numbers. And while Catholics hold a 23% share of these metrics and Evangelical Protestants another 24%, the *vast majority* of these and other Christian churches, congregations, priests, and clergy have absolutely nothing to do with these decadent and avaricious acts, thank God.

Conversely, I'm not blindly upholding the "Nones" to some lofty unimpeachable standard of nobility. Most identify themselves as atheists, agnostics, or "nothing in particular," and all such groups should and must be respected. But one might safely assume that a certain constituency among them has a bone to pick with organized religion ... just because. They are entitled to their views, but they should in turn respect the views of others, including the religious.

Religion does more harm than good when it strays from the only purposes for which it should always be intended—to lead people to God, and to enable people to experience God for themselves. Without this mystical element, religion can devolve into meaningless dogma, a pointless social club, a fanatical cult, a self-serving business venture, or a vehicle to enact political agendas or to sanction hatred and war. The true, undiluted religious experience still exists—at times inside a house of worship, and unceasingly within the silent chamber of one's heart.

To Our Children's Children's Children

Excerpt from website post: December 9, 2021

No, this is not an homage to the Moody Blues' classic 1969 album. But now that the era envisioned by that album's title has occurred, this seems an appropriate time to project into the future when the grandchildren of our present children are growing up, some two generations hence. The following aspirations are from a planetary observer in 2021 to the children of 2071:

The three major biological threats of our present time are still global warming, environmental destruction, and overpopulation. We continue to hope that global warming will be controlled before it's too late. We also hope that we will have preserved more of the pristine environment for you instead of continuing to permit the wholesale destruction of forests, the toxification of oceans, and the disappearance of an alarming number of species, when we clearly could—and should—have chosen another course. We equally hope that we will be able to reduce the rampant population growth of humans. The earth can only handle so many people, and widespread depletion of resources and increased pollution are the result of exceeding these limits.

The combination of runaway commercial interests and short-sighted governmental policies caused these destructive actions, as political powers were corrupted to benefit the forces of commerce. Large-scale apathy by the public allowed this unbridled political–commercial juggernaut to plunder the earth unchecked. As long as our nations place commercial concerns above those of humanity, we will continue spiraling down this slippery slope. And so we pray during this extended holiday season that the dark forces of self-interest be displaced and supplanted by enlightened leaders, working in cooperation with humanity's and the planet's best interests in mind. We hope these conditions are not irreversible, as they often appear to be in 2021.

On a positive note, we hope you are using every means possible to diligently pursue the spiritual path. You have the ability to transform yourselves, and it's only through a complete transformation of your inner being that you can realize your full spiritual potential. Your true nature is unalloyed peace and bliss. Your heart is capable of expressing pure, limitless love. We pray that you don't become ensnared by the world's superficial allurements. Try to see through this facade and seek to unfold your true spiritual nature. It is never too late for this.

No Shortcuts
Website post: March 9, 2023

To PROGRESS SPIRITUALLY, we need to make a passionate commitment to our practice, ideally a lifelong commitment. But there are three caveats.

First, perhaps the most popular misconception about spiritual practice is that no practice is needed. Many times the illusion is promoted that spiritual enlightenment can be attained by intellectual assent, such as merely asserting, *I am already enlightened.* Well, yes, from a nondual perspective, you are already enlightened. But have you truly *realized* this enlightenment in the core of your being? Glib, hollow pronouncements such as "I am already enlightened" when you're really not enlightened constitute armchair mysticism, which is one of the principal ensnarements when walking the spiritual path. You are, in essence, faking your own enlightenment.

Second, it's important not to make spiritual practice something we profess but don't apply in our daily lives. We may label ourselves a follower of this or that faith, but if we don't put the teachings into practice, our allegiance is merely superficial. This defeats the very purpose of following a spiritual path.

Third, we can make spirituality our lifestyle. We may change our name, our clothing, our friends, or our career. Such changes can at times be beneficial, but the danger here is when no real inner transformation takes place. We will have adopted outer changes, but these are merely superficial "lipstick on a pig" modifications that don't affect the core of our being. If this happens, spirituality becomes no more than a hobby.

For spirituality to be effective, it must transform our lives. According to philosopher Gerald Heard, this transformation changes our conduct, character, and our consciousness.[27] Our transformation will be proportionate to the degree we apply ourselves in our practice.

In Hinduism, the Yogasūtra (aphorism 1:22) outlines three degrees of practice—mild, moderate, and intense. The problem is that most modern societies reward material values rather than spiritual values. Productivity, consumption, and progress are esteemed, not navel gazing. It's exceedingly difficult, but not impossible, to practice moderate or intense degrees of spirituality while living in this goal-oriented social environment. One must somehow go against the grain and make an honorable living while at the same time maintain their spiritual focus. But this can and must be done.

In addition, one's psychophysical mechanism—our body and mind—must be conditioned to embody the higher states of consciousness. This normally occurs in deep meditation and takes place over time. Our entire being becomes repeatedly inwardly absorbed in more refined and subtle contemplative states. It is thereby rewired to sustain the deeper levels of spiritual realization. The deep spiritual current then flows throughout our mind and body, interweaving our whole being in a singular, integral matrix of pure spirit.

St. Paul writes, "If there is a natural body, there is also a spiritual body" (1 Cor. 15:44). Some advanced mystics from Christianity and other religious traditions have been so inwardly transformed that they eventually come to reside in and completely identify with their spiritual body—the same as their soul. Their physical body becomes a mere afterthought to these illumined saints; it's like a garment hung on a hanger.

Such transformation can and does take place when we are wholeheartedly devoted to our spiritual practice. This doesn't happen overnight, and it requires sustained effort and no small amount of grace. To effect genuine spiritual transformation in our lives, there are no shortcuts.

Foundations of the Orthodox Church

Excerpt from previously unpublished essay: October 1994

The word *orthodox* is derived from the Greek words *orthos,* meaning "correct" and *doxa,* meaning "belief." Orthodox Christians consider themselves upholders of the "accurate beliefs" of Christianity in its original form, unadulterated by time and subsequent doctrinal modifications.

This is refreshing, because much of what has been called "Christian" over the years, when viewed in the light of Jesus' teachings, is a complete mockery of Christ. Humans create and re-create forms of Christianity that utterly misuse the name of Christ simply to suit their needs and get what they want. But the Christian life calls for a radical inner transformation. As St. Paul wrote in his letter to the Ephesians, "Be renewed mentally and put on a new self, created after the likeness of God ..." (Eph. 4.23–24).

Personal integrity is the cornerstone of any spiritual ethos. The outer indicators of a fruitful inner spiritual life are trustworthiness, reliability, truth, honesty, straightforwardness, and constancy. An individual should demonstrate by their actions a high degree of responsibility, thoughtfulness, courtesy, a modicum of decorum when interacting with others, and flawless accountability when fulfilling obligations. These character traits are expressions of the Golden Rule in practice. Otherwise, ours remains an incomplete realization. People often embrace the relatively superficial elements of religion, such as social reform or philanthropy, without ever undergoing this fundamental inner change. But ethics must proceed hand in hand with mysticism if one's aspiration is to transform their human nature. By doing so, one is able to integrate more spiritual qualities into their character and thereby hoist themselves increasingly upward toward the divine. The effects of such a genuine mystical transformation produce a permanent change in one's behavior. But first, we must create a solid foundation in the very source where such behavior originates—our character. In terms of Christianity, this indeed qualifies as a correct belief.

Inner Justice

Originally published in *Parabola* magazine
Volume 33, No. 4, "Silence," Winter 2008

JUSTICE IS A CONCEPT BASED ON INEQUALITY. A disparity exists that requires balancing in order to restore equity. The gestalt is incomplete; the orphaned fragment must again be made whole.

Compensation is commonly sought for situations involving injustice because they are perceived as unresolved. Once justice is meted out, the process of reparation is viewed as complete. But justice and injustice are, in reality, two sides of one coin. They are part of the cosmic pendulum that swings from justice to injustice, from yin to yang, from *kali yuga* to *satya yuga*. The problem for us is that the pendulum is always in motion. It attains balance but for a moment, only to resume its unending movement through time and space. According to the Vedic Sankhya philosophy, *sattva* (balance) ever interplays with *rajas* (motion) and *tamas* (inertia). Stasis is never permanent. The apparent universe is dynamic and forever changing.

When we encounter injustice, there may be a temporary remedy, a provisional restitution. But this does not mean that the cause has been addressed. The criminal may be behind bars, but the criminal's mindset often remains unchanged. The derelict may win the lottery, but riches cannot buy them sophistication. Similarly, the attainment of justice is often built on illusion.

If we look at the world objectively, without sanitizing what we see, we find that nature is unruly, forever untamed. As Zen Buddhist philosopher Alan Watts observes, it is humans who want to "straighten out a wiggly world."[28] But nature simply *is*, without the embellishments of the many judgmental attributes that humans impute. Consequently, it is we and we alone who discern injustice. And we alone are the ones who demand its recompense. The perception of justice and injustice lies solely within us.

Society has adopted relative determinants of justice and its opposite, which are spread through the fabric of society by means of enculturation. Without such agreed-upon standards, anarchy would reign. So, in the temporal world, these standards, which we call principles, laws, and ethics, are necessary. And so, the Hebrew Bible enjoins, "Keep justice, and do righteousness" (Isa. 56:1).

But when, as Watts further reasons, we mistake these standards for reality, we create a fundamental error.[29] We have, in essence, altered our perception of reality by filtering it through these standards. We then interpret raw experience through the filter, thus circumventing the *suchness* of existence. We believe this filtered experience is real, when in fact it is a representation that has been superimposed on reality. As the Vedanta master Shankara taught, we mistakenly perceive a snake when we have actually encountered a rope.

Vedic philosophy has long posited a profound concept of relativism, *drishti srishti*. The person who views something determines what is seen based on their level of spiritual evolution. In other words, the interpretation of events lies in the eye of the beholder. As Bishop George Berkeley similarly maintained, things are as we perceive them to be. Along these lines, author–philosopher Gerald Heard comments, "Our vision of what we call the Real, we are learning, depends far more on what we have wanted to see, wanted to find, chosen to attend to because it pleased and suited us to see

44

things so, than on what is 'objectively' there."[30] And while there exists an objective reality—the world we daily encounter—Heard reminds us, "This world is but a shadow (though a significant and pressing shadow)."[31]

The world is thus illusory in nature. And because it is ever in flux, it is impermanent. No matter how hard we try to change it to make it appear permanent, if one but gazes intensely on the painting of "reality" we have created, what is revealed is an underlying empty canvas filled in with dabs of fleeting colors. This signifies our futile attempts to create for ourselves a permanent world that conforms to our archetypal dreams of immortality. The canvas of this world momentarily captures our brushstrokes, but they soon wash away. The palette used to create these fleeting images is composed of ever-changing color and light. Any one image is replaced by a succession of new images, all morphing from insubstantiality to emptiness. By grasping at these snapshots of impermanence, we ensure for ourselves a life built on illusion. By trying to make the impermanent permanent, we continually expose our own illusion.

When we encounter injustice, we are in fact witnessing karmic forces emerging from the cosmic depths, breaking into this world of duality. Here they play themselves out—good winning out over bad, evil in turn conquering righteousness. Humans are the unwitting, and all too often willing, pawns of karma. Presuming to act with volitional certitude, we are more frequently mere puppets in the hands of karma, over which we seemingly have little control. Wisdom rests in knowing that the karmic ledgers, and not we, hold the keys to justice. Sooner or later, be it days or centuries or eons, balance will be achieved. That is, until the pendulum again swings in the other direction.

Our duty, therefore, is to attain a state of inner equanimity that is immune to inner and outer change. In such a state, the sense of having achieved balance—and justice—is already attained; the gestalt is always complete. There is no need to arrive at some future circumstance whereby something will be gained in order to offset a perceived deficit. No matter what happens outwardly, we remain unmoved inwardly. Once we experience this state, wherein our inner sense of having attained justice is perpetually secured, we will be far less inclined to react emotionally when we perceive seeming acts of injustice transpire in the outer world.

But how do we achieve this state? By undertaking spiritual practices or what is known in Vedic philosophy as *sadhana*. The purpose of these practices is to situate our awareness in a place where it is impervious to change. This is its original state prior to the process of socialization. Our minds have been conditioned by enculturation, and they must be deconditioned. The deconditioning process is sadhana, which is a systematic foray into the realm of pure consciousness until the pivot point of our being adheres more and more to that elevated realm and we are divested of the superimposed mental flotsam and jetsam that a lifetime of conditioning produces. Sadhana is considered scientific because, if repeated over time, it is expected to yield consistent results.

The end result is a state of equipoise that remains constant despite inner and outer agitations. What at first is routine practice becomes a dawning realization that, over time, unfolds into a visceral, existential apprehension of reality that perceives everything from an entirely different viewpoint than previously experienced. As Swami Vivekananda asserts, "The world will not then be the same world as before."[32] One remains largely unperturbed when confronted with the vacillations of life. Thus, Krishna declares in the Bhagavad Gita, "Unperturbed sameness in all conditions is Yoga" (Gita 2:48).[33]

When we are involved in situations of injustice or inequity, whether social or personal, by maintaining a balanced inner state, we can address them on a more practical and rational level than if we were agitated. We may be wronged or unfairly treated, or we may witness the unfair circumstances that life deals to others, but by maintaining our spiritual bearings we can be calm—centered in the eye of the storm—which is far more productive than reacting emotionally. While it is incumbent on us, at times, to embrace our karmic roles and confront injustice, we must do so without being overtaken by feelings of vengeance or fear. We may in fact react, especially if confronted with a stinging injustice—our landlord sells our rental home out from under us with minimal advance notice; our boss lopsidedly sides with a favored employee when we were fully in the right. But our repeated practice of *sadhana* will imbue us with resiliency and an expanded perspective, which thereby lessens the emotional impact of such incidents to that of water running off a leaf. These circumstances will no longer affect the deep inner level of consciousness where we reside.

Justice and injustice, equity and inequity—these are the pairs of opposites, the *dvandvas* of Sankhya philosophy. In the Bhagavad Gita, Krishna further advises, "Be free from the pair of opposites" (2:45). Both justice and injustice may occur around us or to us, but because we have positioned our awareness in a place that is unaffected by them, we experience these dual principles in an utterly detached manner. The nineteenth-century Indian saint Sri Ramakrishna proclaimed, "God is seen when the mind is tranquil."[34] In that sublime state of deep, unruffled tranquility, we are able to carry with us a preexisting sense of inner justice into all the situations of life we encounter.

Householders – Fighting From Inside a Fort

Excerpt from website post: February 12, 2024,
supplemented by website post (excerpt): January 27, 2024

Ramakrishna likened the householder devotee's life to "fighting from inside a fort." The challenge for householder aspirants is how to maintain one's spiritual bearings both while at home and moving about in the world. It's easy to lose sight of one's spiritual goals because daily life in this country amounts to a 24/7 billboard for commercialism. We're bombarded by commercial enticements around the clock. We worship entertainers, movie stars, sports heroes, billionaires, and the famous, let alone the utterly pointless "celebrities" and "socialites," all of whom frequently dominate the headlines. Forget that many live what we might characterize as dharmically unprofitable lifestyles; the very fact they are rich and famous and bask in their luxurious lives is enough to capture our attention and render us starstruck.

And so, we must prioritize our spiritual goals above *all* other goals and uphold our spiritual attitude, come what may, when interacting with the very secular society in which we live. We must resist getting drawn into the insidious vortex of commercialism and realize that, as with the title of The Police's song, we are but "spirits in the material world." Fame, money, and all ephemeral worldly appellations and knickknacks pass away. God alone exists. *Mementō morī.*

Is There Really a Devil, or Is It Just God in Disguise?

Website post: October 27, 2021 (revised March 2024)

THE SHORT ANSWER to the first part of this question is both yes and no; the answer to the latter part: we certainly hope not! When calamity strikes, oftentimes we can quickly pinpoint the source. If our house gets flooded, the cause might easily be attributed to a river overflowing its banks. But what of those insidious, unexplained, and often vexatious circumstances that cannot offhand be explained? For example, getting stuck sitting next to a chatterbox during a movie, or missing our vacation flight because of gridlock traffic caused by an accident on the way to the airport. Are these situations caused by bad timing, bad luck, or some other instrument of misfortune?

Sometimes we experience periods of setbacks, downturns, and untoward encounters that seemingly cannot be avoided. These circumstances can readily challenge our faith in God. When events really turn bad—a serious illness, losing our job or home—they test our ability to surrender fully to the will of God. While St. Teresa counsels in her well-known Bookmark prayer, "Let nothing disturb you," sometimes this counsel can prove problematic when we are faced with tragedy, illness, or loss, all of which can take the wind out of our sails.

So, who or what is to blame when hardships befall us, especially those that prevent us from getting ahead in life or that sidetrack us from reaching our goals? Relatedly, sometimes we wake up on the wrong side of the bed and nothing seems to go right; everything's out of sync and we're at our wit's end. Who or what is to blame for our bad days? If we profess "Thy will be done"—and actually practice this injunction of Jesus'—we would as a corollary be compelled to believe that God is responsible for all things. But "all things" is sometimes a hard pill to swallow. All things includes bad things, and therein lies the crux of the matter.

Many religions have their version of a demonic influence or entity—Mara (Theravada Buddhism), Satan (Christianity), Iblis (Islam). Still others attribute adversities to malevolent energies (Hinduism, Tibetan Buddhism), which are often portrayed as demons. But, assuming there is a beneficent, omnipotent God, are these demonic influences equally as powerful as God, or are they more powerful than God? If either scenario were true, we'd all be in big trouble.

We would suggest, as do some Eastern religions, that God is one, nondual in nature, and as such, has no counterpart. God is viewed as indivisible in the monotheistic religions as well, though not in a pantheistic sense. According to Hinduism and Buddhism, negative events and what we term "evil" are caused by an impersonal force, karma, and the theory of karma provides a viable explanation for many negative phenomena.

However, within the universe and within us, there exists both positive and negative energies. But to personify the negative energies as possessing power *greater than* God would imply, in the monotheistic religions, that God is not in charge of his own creation. And to personify these negative energies as ultimately possessing power *independent from* God would imply, in certain Eastern religions, that the nondual God is actually dual in nature, thus creating a contradiction.

We might posit that the negative force we term the Devil exists as a power separate from God but ultimately is under God's jurisdiction, as is asserted in the Western biblical traditions. So, like an obnoxious brother-in-law, the Devil, however disconcerting this may seem, is also part of God's household, although he's been consigned to the basement, from where he frequently escapes and, roaming about on earth, "prowls around like a roaring lion, seeking someone to devour" (1 Pet. 5:8).

Still, whether attributable to the Devil or karma, bad things happen in our lives. We could, and should, attempt to banish evil, as Jesus did. We could also, and should also, send waves of compassion to evil forces, as the Dalai Lama does,[35] which parallels what Jesus similarly counseled, "Love your enemies" (Matt. 5:44). And so, whenever we *are* driven to the breaking point and are compelled to shout, "Curse you!" at inimical forces in our lives, we can immediately shout "Bless you!" in the same breath. This has the additional effect of undermining any demonic force that might be plaguing us, because such forces thrive on negativity. By feeding it hatred, it will keep coming back for more. By sending it love, it will starve and thus have no reason to attack us.

In a similar vein, the May 2023, PBS *Nature* episode, "Attenborough's Wonder of Song," demonstrated that bird songs basically convey either one of two messages: *keep away* or *come here*. The challenge for us as spiritual aspirants is to meld both approaches harmoniously when adversity encroaches into our lives.

The Hindu spiritual teacher Sri Ramakrishna (1836–1886) offers a workable solution, by way of a fable–parable. He related a tale wherein a holy man teaches a venomous snake the ways of nonviolence (*ahimsa*). He warns the slithering creature not to harm anyone. But after the now-passive snake is beaten by some cowherd boys, the holy man chastises it for not *hissing* to keep potential attackers away. "You should hiss at bad people to frighten them so they don't harm you," Ramakrishna advised, "but you must not inject poison into others and injure them."[36]

Once we reconcile ourselves with our fate and accept the presence of negative events in our lives, we are better poised to rise above both good and evil, and look upon these twin forces, as does Taoism, with an unperturbed mind while gracefully remaining in a state of surrender as the storms of life rage around us. One very helpful watchword to remember when caught up in a given storm: "Let nothing disturb you."

A More Permanent Lenten Abstinence
Excerpt from website post: March 27, 2023

If we analyze our nature by peeling apart our identity, we can see that our sense of "I" is used simply as a point of reference to distinguish between us and other people or things that exist apart from us. Yet, we can and routinely do acquire an overly developed sense of the importance of our "I," and that's where the problem starts. It is a healthy part of one's individuation process to possess a well-rounded sense of identity—knowing who we are in the world and in relation to others. But when we cling too much to our "I" and its multitudinous desires and attachments, we become beholden to strong surges of emotional reactions that sway us to and fro. These reactions carry us away from our spiritual base.

We are not the "I" we think we are. There exists within us a spiritual component—our spiritual self—that transcends our secular persona. We can contact this spiritual element, which is our true nature, through dedicated spiritual practice. Eventually, we come to identify with our spiritual self more than our secular self. Unlike our secular persona, our spiritual self is forever unchanging, blissful, peaceful, and not subject to the vacillations of time and space. This is our true identity.

During Lent, and every day throughout the year, we can put our secular self on a diet by abstaining from thoughts, words, and actions that are based in ego, greed, selfishness, anger, and all negative emotions. We can empower and strengthen our spiritual self by undertaking spiritual practices that put us in touch with it: prayer, meditation, devotion, surrender, altruism. In this way, we bring about a permanent transformation within ourselves. Such a transformation will abide with us well beyond this holy Lenten season.

Madness … or Gratitude
Website post: November 23, 2021

IN A CLASSIC UNDERGROUND ANIMATION SHORT from the early 1970s, Planet Earth is shown from afar as voicing the collective demands of humanity by shouting, via speech bubbles, "more" … then "More" … then even "MORE." Finally, at the end of this temper tirade, the hand of God reaches out and crushes the planet, destroying the earth in a split second. God then gets the final word: "No more!"

This prophetic little cartoon graphically depicts our current, woeful state of affairs on Planet Earth, short of the apocalyptic final scene, which at least for now is on hold. In our modern Western world, "more" is the mantra for our day-to-day secular lives. Consume more, get more. Never stop consuming, never stop acquiring.

And what are we consuming and acquiring? Things. Possessions. Stuff. Ephemeral trinkets and shiny bric-a-brac. Fancy cars and smart homes. All sorts of external adornments, artificial exoskeletons, and transitory pleasures of the senses.

But this insatiable lust for temporal enhancements has come at a cost. Unless God gets fed up with his creation, his intervention won't be required to deal the final, fateful hand to humanity. Planet Earth has been belching NO MORE for decades, and now we are at the tipping point. Global warming, climate change, ecological decline, environmental destruction, extinction of many species, overpopulation, overcrowding: we have long been forewarned about the deleterious effects of blindly empowering commercial interests while ignoring our planet's collective interests. But have we been listening?

In contrast to our unbridled consumerism and its detrimental environmental impacts is the concept of voluntary simplicity advanced by philosopher Henry David Thoreau (1817–1862). This idea places reins on unlimited avariciousness, which is a kind of madness. However, as we prepare to celebrate Thanksgiving, the idea of being content with one's circumstances and grateful for one's lot in life seems somewhat blasé, almost anachronistic in today's gimme-gimme world. Yet, from a spiritual point of view, contentment and gratitude are as much food for the soul as is even the most humble Thanksgiving meal.

We leave this life in the same way we enter it: possessionless. Thus, it would behoove us to remember, as we accrue more and more barnacles of possessions throughout our lives, that in the end, there simply is no more. As we travel on our spiritual journey, we can view our temporal possessions as items on loan to us to help further our spiritual development. And we can always be grateful. Especially on this year's Thanksgiving Day remembrance.

Confession: Good for the Soul
Website post: February 27, 2022

SO, WHAT IS MEANT BY "CONFESSION"? The word *confession* is derived from the Latin *confessiō* meaning "to admit." Making a confession presupposes someone has something to admit. In terms of a person walking the spiritual path, there is always plenty to admit. But not simply a litany of one's transgressions, follies, or shortcomings. True confession shines a light on what is hidden in one's mind: the impulses that drive us. These impulses include the habit patterns we act out, the kneejerk behaviors we display, and the emotions we express. In other words, everything that makes us tick.

Normally, we are not aware of these impulses, patterns, and behaviors, and we are frequently puppets of our emotions. This is because these items lurk as unconscious elements in our minds. Yet, they often lead us by the nose throughout our lives. They act as obstacles that block our goal of enlightenment. And so, we seek liberation from these unconscious, mechanical forces that seemingly dictate our responses, control our lives, and sheep-hook us in every which way, often against our better judgment.

Accordingly, it is critical to engage in the kind of ongoing self-examination that confession implies. By looking inside our own mind, we can see beyond our behavior and pinpoint what truly motivates us. Generally, a person's mind is not always a repository of spiritual treasures, but a jumble of emotions, memories of the past, plans for the future, and a serious admixture of wants and needs.

I once heard a Tibetan lama say words to the effect that a toilet bowl can be cleaner than the contents of our minds. He wasn't joking. Notwithstanding all the good thoughts we have, just try to count the number of bad thoughts that arise in a given day.

A good litmus test is to see how many negative emotions you display within, say, a half-hour's time. Did you lose your patience? Express anger? Or maybe not fully tell the truth? If you ask yourself these questions, you are engaging in confession. You are admitting that various emotions had overtaken your mind, which caused you to act or react in ways that may be contrary to your spiritual values.

By first identifying then admitting such things to oneself, an aspirant makes progress at overcoming these very same driving forces within themselves. This is the first step toward unshackling oneself from their influence. Once sufficiently loosened, they no longer hold sway over us. We then attain a kind of self-mastery, which is an essential trait as we proceed along the path of enlightenment. Confession thus allows a person to see into their often-recalcitrant mind and free themselves from its clutches. What lies beyond is one's soul or spiritual self. Once the soul is plainly in view, we'll then clearly see how confession has served its ennobling purpose.

The Narrow Gate
Website post: March 29, 2022

Enter through the narrow gate. For wide is the gate and broad is the path that leads to destruction, yet many enter through it. But small is the gate and narrow the path that leads to life, and only a few ever find it.

–Matthew 7:13–14

THESE ENIGMATIC WORDS OF JESUS lend themselves to different interpretations. Jesus used an analogy, as he so often did when explaining spiritual truths. His profound words here can be viewed as both cautionary and encouraging.

For a spiritual aspirant, Jesus' message can be interpreted on two levels: exoteric and esoteric. In terms of the former, a legitimate spiritual path will lead to "life"; that is, it will lead to God, to spiritual illumination. Any such path will always be small and narrow—not for the masses, but for the few. And typically, such a path requires that we undergo transformations which result in a change to our conduct and character. When we are enlightened, we will not be the same person we are now. And so, we must commit ourselves whole-heartedly to our path, whatever our circumstances in life. If we are serious, we will shed unproductive behaviors and negative mindsets along our journey. But this vital inner work should not be viewed as some kind of melancholy drudgery. St. Teresa of Ávila advised, "God save us from gloomy saints!" We would be wise to follow her savvy counsel.

On an esoteric level, some spiritual traditions posit the existence of a subtle body, which is said to be the unseen counterpart to one's physical body. This concept is familiar to anyone who has under-gone acupuncture treatment, which works on meridians that are in-visible to the eye but which are viewed as part of one's subtle body. Many energy-healing modalities attempt to achieve therapeutic wholeness by working on the subtle body.

Within one's subtle body, some traditions based in India further theorize there is an intense spiritual energy, known as *kundalini*, which, when awakened by spiritual practices, ascends through a sub-tle, small, narrow energy channel located inside the spine called the *sushumna nadi*. This is identical with the Central Meridian in Tradi-tional Chinese Medicine. I believe this spiritual energy has similarities with *Shekhinah* in Kabbalism and the Holy Spirit in Christian doctrine. When awakened, it must pierce several knots along its upward spinal ascent, until it reaches the top of the crown where it confers unimag-ined dimensions of ecstasy that ripple through the dazed aspirant. Now, it is certainly a stretch to assume or even infer that Jesus meant all this. Still, this inner esoteric process has a parallel that could be interpreted as corresponding to Jesus' words.

Circling back to our exoteric interpretation, if we don't enter through the narrow gate—the path that leads to God—we're basically wasting our human life, hence we are on the opposite path, the path that leads to destruction. In other words, we're not making any sig-nificant spiritual progress, which is the purpose of life.

Two paths: narrow leading to life, and wide leading to destruc-tion. The former leads to spiritual illumination, while traipsing along the latter signifies a conscious forfeiture of our opportunity for spiritual advancement. Which path will we walk?

Vesak – Honoring the Buddha
Website post: May 8, 2022

STARTING TODAY AND CONTINUING ON VARIOUS DAYS over the next week, Buddhists throughout the world commemorate the birth, enlightenment, and death of Prince Siddhartha Gautama—the Buddha—on a day of great celebration and joy known as Vesak. But we must ask: Which Buddha is honored on this day? The answer depends on which branch of Buddhism does the celebrating.

In the Theravada tradition, the historical Buddha is honored. In Mahayana Buddhism, one encounters the doctrine of Buddha's three bodies (*Trikaya*), where Gautama is honored as a physical personification of the *Nirmanakaya*, or "appearance" body of the cosmic Buddha. In Tibetan Buddhism, the *Nirmanakaya* is equated with the *Vajra* body of the Buddha, symbolizing the abstract ideal of indestructible pure actions. Thus, every tradition perceives Buddha in a different light.

But even more significant is how Gautama's enlightenment is viewed. In each of the main schools of Buddhism, his illumination becomes increasingly expanded—from having attained *nirvāṇa* in the Theravada school; to becoming an all-compassionate bodhi-sattva who postpones his own enlightenment until all beings are liberated in the Mahayana lineages; to the Tibetan concept of becoming a bodhisattva then further unfolding an all-encompassing transcendent nondual Awareness composed of wisdom, compassion, and indescribable bliss.

And so, practitioners in each tradition will attain the type of enlightenment propounded by each path. One might casually conclude that one path builds upon the other, as some Tibetan Buddhists maintain. But in practical terms, each path is complete unto itself, without the need of such a hierarchical structure. It would be a slight to suggest to a dedicated Theravada monk that their practice is deficient because it lacks the trademark Mahayana element of unlimited compassion. The concept of *metta* or lovingkindness is enjoined throughout Theravada teachings as one of the Ten Perfections. If one is drawn to the more esoteric Tibetan practices, that practitioner will attain results according to their dedication and the intensity of their practice. Thus, each branch is suitable and wholly appropriate for a variety of practitioners based on their innate temperament, proclivities, and aptitude.

But none of this would be possible without the historical personage to whom Vesak is dedicated—Prince Siddhartha. The worldwide Vesak celebrations this week pay homage to the founder of one of the world's great paths to enlightenment.

What's With The Ball?
Website post: December 11, 2023

AN ONGOING MATTER I'VE LONG FOUND DISCONCERTING really caught my attention last weekend. It deals with The Ball. No, not the Times Square Ball, which descends in New York City every New Year's Eve to mark the start of the new year. I'm referring to none other than the ubiquitous sports ball, be it a golf ball, basketball, tennis ball, football, soccer ball, volleyball, or baseball, to list some of the more popular spectator sports that are based on using The Ball. Less commonly, this includes a bowling ball, ping pong ball, or even variations such as a puck or a shuttlecock, and also a rugby ball or cricket ball if a game is predominately played outside the United States. There are numerous other ball games. But here's the rub.

The December 9, 2023, headline from CBS Sports read as follows: *Shohei Ohtani becomes world's highest-paid athlete after signing lucrative contract with Dodgers.* That contract is worth $700 million—that's *seven hundred million dollars*—over 10 years (technically, 20 years when counting "luxury tax" deferrals).

Now, reliable sources date the advent of homo sapiens back to around 200,000 years ago. Evidence of sports events date from around 15,000 B.C. to 10,000 B.C. So, competitive sports are a longstanding part of recent human activity, relatively speaking.

In terms of The Ball, with sufficient training a person can acquire a knack to throw it, catch it, toss it into a hoop, kick it between goalposts, putt it into a hole, or bat it out of a ballpark. There have been superstar players in each sport in the past, and there will be such players in the future. But somewhere along the line, these skillful players became grossly overpaid to the point of obscenity.

No, I'm not going off on an anti-capitalism rant. But I am in complete agreement with one article from the *Intelligencer* that called this contract "insane."[37] And, I might add, shamelessly appalling. Paying anyone $700 million, let alone $100 million or $_____ (fill in your breakpoint figure) to hit, kick, catch, or dunk a moving ball reflects what we value as a society. And, of course, money is Number One. And unquestionably, the more the better.

The top five highest paid athletes of all time are listed below (source: *The Bleacher Report*,[38] which I've adapted):

–Shohei Ohtani, baseball: 10 years, $700 million
–Lionel Messi, soccer: 4 years, $674 million
–Patrick Mahomes, football: 10 years, $450 million
–Mike Trout, baseball: 12 years, $426.5 million
–Karim Benzema, soccer: 2 years, $426 million

Now, I'm not trashing these players. But I'll simply contrast their exorbitant salaries with the three photographs from recent years on the opposite page, which show some children whose families likely did not possess as much money as these athletes, and who may not exactly be laughing all the way to the bank each day. And certainly, we should not anticipate any children currently living in similar circumstances playing professional sports with The Ball anytime soon.

Photo credits from top to bottom:

1. *Grayscale Photo of an Innocent Child* by Hamza Awan (2022), licensed for free usage, via Pixabay. / Resized.
2. *Children, Slums, Poverty* by billycm (2017), licensed for free usage, via Pixabay. / Resized.
3. *Slums, India, Poverty* by billycm (2019), licensed for free usage, via Pixabay. / Resized.

Religious Nationalism
Excerpt from website post: September 29, 2022

A recent headline caught my attention, about certain factions that support declaring the United States a Christian nation. This is a seriously flawed idea. Any kind of religious nationalism, which by definition means the ruling political body exclusively aligns with a particular religion (and its interpretation of that religion) to the exclusion of others, then imposes that religion on all, is anathema to the very concept of democracy. Religious nationalism is a form of autocracy, not to mention elitism, and elitism is based on inequality, prejudice, and discrimination, not egalitarianism, while autocracy is a form of dictatorship.

Beyond that, let's examine the idea of Christian nationalism in light of the teachings of the man whose name the Christian religion bears. Religious nationalism is predicated on eliminating the separation of church and state. However, Jesus upheld this separation, stating, "Render to Caesar the things that are Caesar's, and to God the things that are God's" (Mark 12:17). The proponents of Christian nationalism often support a doctrine of exclusivity and isolation from others. Whereas Jesus taught a gospel of selfless love. This entails hands-on involvement with and unlimited liability toward one's fellow human beings. Yes, we are our human siblings' keepers (see Gen. 4:9). Some Christian nationalists express vitriol toward certain races or classes of people. Whereas Jesus taught us to love one another unconditionally.

Thus, some of those professing Christian nationalism espouse beliefs that profoundly contradict the unambiguous teachings imparted by Jesus. It is incumbent on us not to even remotely confuse such regressive credos with the true message of Jesus. Those extremists who promote such positions pollute Jesus' teachings of universal love and peace, and they superficially use Christianity to advance their own agenda of animosity and divisiveness.

For those who are enamored of establishing the United States as a Christian-only nation, please cease and desist. For those claiming to be Christian but who actually despise certain others, please leave true Christianity alone and keep your own religion of hate to yourselves. Even better, renounce all malice and ill-will and strive to embody the boundless love that Jesus taught.

The Ultimate Path

Previously unpublished essay: April 2009

Two birds, inseparable friends, cling to the same tree. One of them eats the fruit of divergent tastes, the other looks on without eating.[39]

–Mundaka Upanishad 3:1:1

EVERY PATH LEADS TO A DESTINATION; every voyage arrives at a terminus point. There are many journeys in life for us to travel, many routes for us to traverse. There are those in the outer sphere of life, such as the intertwined journeys we tread with our families, our relatives, our colleagues, and our circle of friends. There are paths we explore that enrich our inner world, such as our intellectual pursuits and those which further our spiritual unfoldment. Whenever we fall in love, read a novel, or embrace a new goal in life, we embark on a path. Whether our aim is to finish college, raise children, advance in our career, or learn a new craft, we set out on new pathways in order to accomplish a certain goal. We then equip ourselves with the skills and means necessary to complete our journey. And, most important, we position ourselves to succeed when we fuel our expedition with enthusiasm, passion, and a dogged determination to achieve our goal.

Among the many paths we travel, the spiritual path is our most personal. Though we're not always aware of this, our spirituality lies at the core of every path we walk. This is because each action we take and decision we make reflects our spiritual makeup. However, our spiritual nature is often buried under layers of acquired emotional reactions and ingrained character traits. Thus, we frequently function as automatons, at the mercy of unconscious processes, habits, and impulses. Unless we intentionally choose to evolve our level of spirituality, our habitual patterns and deep-rooted reactions will continue to influence our lives. By opting to develop ourselves spiritually, we are better able to regulate our own pace of spiritual evolution and gradually undo these rigid patterns.

When walking a spiritual path, many avenues abound for us to follow. Some persons are drawn to religious services, charitable works, pilgrimages, penances, scriptural studies, devotional hymns, chanting, and so forth. Yet, there is one spiritual path that more directly propels us toward an encounter with the ultimate reality or God. This is known as mysticism—the branch of philosophy which asserts that the ultimate reality can be personally experienced. This mystical component is a foundational element of all transformational spiritual paths, and the mystical path is the most significant path we will travel in our life.

According to the Vedanta tradition, the mystical journey consists of reducing the gap between our outer self (*jiva*)—our ego, character, and personality—and our innermost spiritual self (*atman*) until our outer self is completely eclipsed. Whether a person consciously seeks to walk the mystical path or whether they stumble onto it as a serendipitous byproduct of their devotional or contemplative practices, the underlying thrust of our spiritual endeavors is to reconnect with our spiritual self, with God.

But, similar to Dorothy's plight in *The Wonderful Wizard of Oz*, we tend to forget one important fact. We all too often mistakenly seek our spiritual self in any number of places outside ourselves. A person may attend church or participate in religious study groups, seminars, workshops, and retreats. These activities may very well provide camaraderie and furnish noteworthy revelations along our journey. But momentary epiphanies, however profound, do not produce a permanent transformation in our innermost being. To retain whatever gains we make on our spiritual journey, we must undertake spiritual practices that are consistently and diligently applied, and which help us to realize our goal. And, as Dorothy discovered, the goal is and has always been within us.

We often, though, encounter resistance along our spiritual path, sometimes even distaste toward our practices. Adept practitioners and spiritual directors from all traditions have commented on these dry spells. They are part of the ebb and flow of one's spiritual life, and they have affected aspirants and devotees as varied as Ramakrishna, St. Teresa of Ávila, Job, and Milarepa. When undergoing a dry spell, the remedy is to ease up a bit on our practices and persevere with less rigor for a time. Remember this too shall pass. But also be aware there is danger of backsliding if we slacken off too much.

However, when the spiritual doldrums set in for a prolonged period and produce a formidable bout of resistance, there is a possibility that a kind of defeatist malaise will take hold. This can turn a once-blossoming practice into a sabotaging malady. A seemingly overpowering force tries to prevent us from pursuing our practices. Our spiritual resolve dies a slow death with each passing day. Soon a month or more has passed, and what was once a passionate embrace of spirituality is often tragically abandoned, perhaps seen in retrospect as nothing more than a passing fad.

Yet, it's useful to know that this resistance is actually part of the spiritual process. Spiritual practice is purgative; it dislodges the nonproductive fragments inside us that prevent us from unfolding our spiritual self. It's a spring-cleaning of the psyche. The stagnant pond of the conditioned, habituated mind receives a fresh supply of uncontaminated spiritual water, and all the accumulated muck gets stirred up and pushed downstream—out of our being—leaving a clear, purified reservoir of pristine spirituality in its place.

And so, over the course of time, spiritual practice agitates our embedded mental patterns, which include occasional spells of resistance toward the very practice we undergo. Eventually, all such patterns are purged, thus releasing their grip on us. In his Yogasūtra (aphorism

1:30), the Indian sage Patanjali lists inertia, doubt, and lack of enthusiasm—all synonymous with resistance—among the mental distractions that serve as obstacles to realizing our spiritual goal. We should be attentive to these psychological barriers when they arise, and be patient with ourselves and especially adroit when dealing with them.

Another issue we face is when external situations, usually negative, seemingly manifest out of nowhere and divert us from our goal. Whether they be illness, financial difficulties, a family emergency, or, equally seriously, a layoff from work or even homelessness, worldly circumstances arise that demand our time, attention, and energy. Tending to these situations can easily shift our spiritual focus. If we cooperate by reacting to such circumstances and emotionally participating with them, they will have gained the upper hand by toppling us from our spiritual base.

Walking the path of spirituality can be the most challenging task before us. Reconnecting with our spiritual self requires us to constantly renew our commitment to our goal and reaffirm our spiritual values. This also means we must avoid becoming engulfed by the distractions that arise in our lives. Various trying circumstances will always occur, so when navigating them we must never lose sight of our most important goal, which is experiential mystical realization.

The Bengal-based Sufi saint Sharafuddin Maneri (1263–1381) related the following story. "Someone asked a saint: 'What is an idol?' The saint replied, 'Whatever diverts you from God is your idol.' "[40] It benefits all aspirants to view life's adverse circumstances not as obstacles, but as *part* of their spiritual journey. Our day-to-day interactions act as a laboratory where our spiritual practice is tested. By spiritualizing everything in life, we will never get sidetracked.

For those of us living in the world as householders, the path before us, then, is no more and no less than our everyday life—whatever presents itself from waking to sleeping, from diapers to dishes, from home to work. It is said in Buddhist circles that the most important part of meditation is when you rise up from your meditation cushion. Ideally one's practice never stops, so there should be no arbitrary line of demarcation between sitting in meditation and engaging in activity afterward. Over time, we are able to maintain a thread of continuity throughout the waking state with the deeper spiritual dimension we access during meditation. We will come to realize, as did the Parisian Carmelite Brother Lawrence (1611–1691), who served as the monastery cook, that, "The set times of prayer were not different from other times."[41] Lawrence further amazingly stated, "The time of business ... does not with me differ from the time of prayer; and in the noise and clatter of my kitchen, while several persons are at the same time calling for different things, I possess God in as great tranquility as if I were upon my knees at the blessed sacrament."[42]

What creates difficulties for us are our attachments—our likes and dislikes, desires, prejudices, and reactions. We become preoccupied with gain, and we painstakingly shun loss. This is simply human nature—to desire good and avoid bad—for which we cannot be faulted. It's when we become fixated on gain or loss that the trouble begins. As with the first allegorical bird of Upanishadic lore that "eats the fruit of divergent tastes" in life, our outer self gets caught in a world of flux, vacillating between swirling emotions of love and hate, sorrow and joy. Whereas our spiritual self altogether transcends these fluctuations and "looks on without eating," as does the wiser second bird. Our spiritual self—our true nature—is the second bird: the eternal witness, forever unattached to the events of life, ever liberated, and perpetually immersed in transcendent bliss.

The ultimate path is whichever path we follow that unfolds our spiritual self, which in reality is ever-present and ever-luminous, existing within us at all times. Treading the spiritual path can often challenge us to the core. The world is designed to engage our attention, and our secular life typically consists of a series of never-ending obligations. But, by forging ahead undaunted and rallying ourselves to attain our goal, we can mobilize our efforts toward undoing our fossilized mental patterns. We persevere during dry spells, cope with mental distractions that arise, and embrace all external situations as part of our path. We will thereby be using skillful means to help effect a permanent transformation in our psyches, which opens the door to our pure consciousness within. We will, like the wise second bird, calmly observe the events of life while remaining inwardly detached, all the while suffused with the scintillating presence of our deep unbroken spiritual realization, which is the ultimate fruit of our having skillfully traversed the spiritual path.

On the Shore of Walden Pond

Excerpt from lecture delivered at the Friends of the Spirit
study group in Redding, California: June 4, 1987

The great American philosopher and naturalist Henry David Thoreau, a highly sensitive and intelligent man, was peeved that most people— perhaps not so sensitive or intelligent—should live like "machines" and not concern themselves with philosophy or devote their lives to more noble ends than those gained by "coarse labors." Many people indeed lead lives of "quiet desperation," yet, "it is a characteristic of wisdom not to do desperate things."[43] Such real-life observations have often been the despair of abstract philosophers. Further, why should Thoreau's ironic and slightly cynical reflections attract the attention of a world that is weary of pessimism and complaint?

Because—and this was Thoreau's genius—he set out to answer his own criticism by *changing his mode of life*. He did not take up the course followed by most philosophers, which is to promulgate a system of abstruse metaphysics, and which, in essence, is totally divorced from the reality of daily life. Daily life *was* his metaphysics; "the present moment," his truest reality. "God himself culminates in the present moment," he declared.[44] All else is speculation and gibberish designed, perhaps, by pompous boors to impress other pompous boors.

"There are nowadays professors of philosophy, but not philosophers. ... To be a philosopher is not merely to have subtle thoughts, nor even to found a school, but to so love wisdom as to live according to its dictates, a life of simplicity, independence, magnanimity, and trust. It is to solve some of the problems of life, not only theoretically, but practically."[45] Thus spoke a true philosopher's philosopher.

Merging With the Infinite
Website post: June 6, 2022

IN HINDUISM'S VEDANTA PHILOSOPHY, the ultimate reality is often referred to as *Satchitananda*. This Sanskrit term is wonderfully descriptive, as it includes three inseparable and interrelated attributes of Brahman, or God, in the context of Hinduism: (1) *Sat*, or the underlying essence of all things; (2) *Chit*, or pure consciousness; and (3) *Ananda*, or supernal bliss. Thus, the ultimate reality is the essence of everything in the universe and is inherently composed of consciousness and bliss.

Our encounter with the ultimate reality must be subjective, personal, and direct. Everything else is speculative and based on secondhand accounts, however helpful they may be.

Through our own determined pursuit of enlightenment, we can merge with the Infinite. *Satchitananda* not only describes the nature of the ultimate reality, but it also describes our subjective experience of it. In the deepest states of inner contemplation, our mind and emotions are stilled, and our sense of individuality, or ego, comes to a halt. In this limitless space, we are able to encounter the ultimate reality, which is omnipresent and therefore found within us.

However, when we initially experience this reality, we perceive it as existing apart from us. But over the course of time, if our practice sessions go deep enough, we lose this awareness of separation. This is because we merge with it. Or rather, our ego is splintered off and left behind as our awareness merges with the ultimate reality. Thus, *Sat* (the essence of reality) and *Chit* (our own pure consciousness, sans the ego) are united into one, and this union confers unimaginable cascading torrents of ineffable *Ananda* or bliss, which bathes our inner being in paradisiacal ecstasies. We can eventually experience this same oneness and bliss during activity.

There are different theories that account for the arising of *Ananda,* or bliss. According to Vedanta theory, the spiritual self or *atman* is covered by five *koshas,* or sheaths. The innermost *kosha* is the *Anandamaya kosha,* or the sheath of bliss. During deep contemplation, the aspirant's awareness gravitates toward the sheath of bliss, which is situated in closest proximity to the *atman,* their spiritual self. And so, because of this adjacency, the devotee is bathed in streams of pure bliss that emanate from the sheath of bliss. Once they transcend their ego, they merge with their radiant spiritual self and become one with this inner bliss.

Other Eastern religious theories attribute this bliss to the awakening of the *kundalini,* the profound inner spiritual energy that is said to lie dormant within us all. Still other theories, such as those that underscore Taoist esoteric practices or the secret Tantra methods of Tibetan Buddhism, ascribe different causes.

It is eminently possible to contact the ultimate reality and to be transformed by this contact, as mystics throughout the ages have demonstrated. Our goal in life is to merge with the Infinite. By doing so, we shed our finite human qualities and realize our true infinite nature.

Mahayana Buddhism and the Gunas

Website post: July 10, 2023

MAHAYANA ("THE GREAT VEHICLE") BUDDHISM is one of the principal branches of Buddhism. Two major traditions derive from the Mahayana: the Tantrayana of Tibet, or Tibetan Buddhism; and the Chan, more widely known as Zen.

Unlike the orthodox Theravada ("the Way of the Elders") tradition, which is Buddhism's third main branch, Mahayana Buddhism emphasizes the path of the bodhisattva. Practitioners vow not to attain personal enlightenment until all sentient beings are enlightened. To facilitate this magnanimous goal, aspirants cultivate an attitude of *bodhichitta*, which is a loving, patient, compassionate, sympathetic—almost motherly—attitude toward all. The XIV Dalai Lama frequently mentions during his live webcasts that he generates this attitude every morning when he awakes. To quote him, "Everyone is my friend."[46]

I believe him! This is the Mahayana Buddhist equivalent to Jesus' injunction for us to "love one another" (John 13:34). St. Paul also emphasizes this theme (Eph. 4:32, Col. 3:12). This world provides enough daily examples of people hating one another, so it is encouraging to have these spiritual giants advocating the opposite.

Next, we'll take a thumbnail overview of the Hindu concept of the *gunas*, which is prominently featured in the Vedic philosophical school known as Sankhya. Gunas are the qualities or states in which a given thing—from foods to states of mind to the state of the cosmos—can be classified. There are three gunas—*tamas* (inertia or stasis), *rajas* (activity or motion), and *sattva* (equilibrium or balance).

In the context of spiritual evolution, a *tamasic* person could be a materialist, an atheist, a secular humanist, or even a rigid religious dogmatist. In any event, they are often stuck at the lower rungs of spiritual evolution as they are largely unmotivated to make significant spiritual progress in this life. A *rajasic* adherent, on the other hand, engages in *sadhana* (spiritual disciplines), and thereby consciously attempts to accelerate their own spiritual evolution. A *sattvic* aspirant, having engaged in practice for years or even decades, is able to "taste" a certain degree of illumination by virtue of their personal experience.

This same guna classification holds true of practices undertaken by different aspirants. Tamasic adherents may practice the grosser forms of worship—for example, animal (or human, as we have seen in some cultures!) sacrifice. Rajasic aspirants turn rosary beads, participate in rituals and ceremonies, and so forth. Sattvic aspirants may meditate or perform devotional exercises, which are more interior. Circling back to our Mahayana Buddhist discussion, one such sattvic practice is generating bodhichitta—universal love for all.

However, there is a state that transcends the gunas. In the Bhagavad Gita, the *avatar* Krishna enjoins his bewildered disciple Arjuna to "rise above the gunas" (Gita 2:45). This is the same as the closely related concept of *trigunatita*—the state wherein one transcends the influence of the gunas, which occurs in the higher stages of spiritual development. At first, the aspirant catches glimpses of this exalted state. But with repeated practice, a tangible sense of realization becomes increasingly integrated into their being.

With this background, I can now introduce my main point. Is the Mahayana ideal of maintaining an attitude of bodhichitta preferable to the Vedic concept of transcending the gunas? In other words, should an aspirant continually uphold their sattvic attitude of love and compassion, or go beyond sattva to the ultimate experience of enlightenment, which is devoid of all such qualities?

Oh, but were this a dilemma faced by us! First, are we even in a sattvic state? Do we feel a continuous flow of loving thoughts toward all? Have we really attained a state of equipoise wherein we don't react when others harm us? Do we "love your enemies and pray for those who persecute you" (Matt. 5:44)? What if we encounter those whose lifestyles or politics meet with our disapproval? What about convicted murderers, terrorists, abusers, or torturers? The crimes they commit are heinous, but can we love their inner spiritual essence unconditionally while neutrally, unemotionally condemning their outer actions? This is where the rubber hits the road. Our hearts must be purged of the last remnants of malice and ill-will, unreservedly, without exception. This is sattva.

So again, once we attain this state of universal love toward all beings—which is not merely glib talk or abstract theory—is it better to maintain this state continuously or transcend it and dive headlong into the attributeless void of the ultimate reality? By holding on to even the thought of love, one is creating a groove in one's mind—a *samskara*. Because of this, the mind cannot be fully transcended; all such grooves must be entirely surmounted in order to attain full-blown liberation.

What do the great teachers say? In the very same sutra where Krishna advises transcending the gunas, he *also* counsels, "always remain in the quality of sattva" (Gita 2:45). The Dalai Lama routinely advocates that we maintain an ongoing attitude of bodhichitta *combined with* the practice of emptiness. If you take Jesus' injunction, "Seek first the kingdom of God" (Matt. 6:33), *along with* his counsel for us to "love your neighbor as yourself" (Mark 12:31), there you have it. These different teachers all agree that we should focus our efforts on attaining a continuous loving attitude—a sattvic state—while *simultaneously* aspiring toward the highest spiritual realization that we will achieve once the gunas are transcended. In fact, when we become enlightened, our thoughts and actions automatically take on predominantly sattvic qualities. At that heightened stage in our development, we both walk the precipice and take the final plunge into the abyss at the same time.

His Holiness the XIV Dalai Lama

Excerpt from website post: July 27, 2022

I had traveled to meet or study with the Dalai Lama three times. During one empowerment I attended in San Francisco in the late 1990s, I recall a split second during the preliminary stages of the event, presided over by His Holiness, when suddenly a palpable shift took place, akin to a spiritual sonic boom, as though a fissure abruptly occurred in the time-space continuum and powerful supernal blessings were released that rippled through the assembly.

Another such occasion took place on June 27, 1993. Through connections, I stood in a line where the Dalai Lama personally greeted each of us after consecrating an Avalokitesvara sand mandala at the Art Gallery of Greater Victoria, B.C. Then came my turn in line, and sure enough, there he stood right before me. After offering him a *katha* (white scarf), His Holiness in turn placed it around my neck—a traditional observance—as I stood with my head bowed before him and my hands joined together in respectful salutation. But I neglected to open my eyes! After several seconds, I suddenly felt compelled to open them, and there he was, staring right into my eyes, into the very depths of my being, from about a foot away, his face beaming his inimitable smile. Then he broke into his characteristic deep, bellowing, contagious laughter, all the while gazing deep into my eyes. I smiled back. I guarantee, time stood still during this once-in-a-lifetime experience. He then moved on to the next person.

However, during those few magical moments, something happened inside me. I had to sequester myself in a quiet room for perhaps 15 minutes. There I sat on the floor, absorbing a torrential influx of mindboggling spiritual energy, which affected me on the deepest of levels. His Holiness' blessing was so powerful that I could not function for some time. To this day, I am placed in that same profound spiritual mood whenever I recall my brief but extraordinarily intense encounter with him, which would not have occurred had I not closed my eyes for so long. Indeed, the Dalai Lama opened my eyes, not only literally, but also figuratively, as his inspired, impromptu blessing enabled me to experience a gapingly unfathomable dimensionless spiritual realm.

Jesus' Post-Crucifixion Appearances
Website post: April 6, 2023

ACCORDING TO THE GOSPEL ACCOUNTS, Jesus of Nazareth died on Good Friday, then rose on Easter Sunday. The narratives relate that Jesus was resurrected from the dead. In the New Testament, we find eleven instances of Jesus' appearances from Easter Sunday until forty days later when we read of his final earthly appearance in Bethany, where the Gospels state that he ascended into heaven.

When we read the exact descriptions of Jesus' post-crucifixion appearances, we find two common themes: (1) most of his intimate followers who knew Jesus very well while he was alive barely recognized him; (2) many times he suddenly appeared, seemingly out of thin air. I'll cite examples from the New Testament that support these two themes.

Two women named Mary visited Jesus' tomb on Easter Sunday (Matt. 28:1). Mary Magdalene, who first saw him, "did not realize that it was Jesus" (John 20:14).[47] She thought he was a gardener! Presumably, she reverentially bowed, either embracing or intending to embrace his feet. But Jesus cryptically told her, "Do not hold on to me, for I have not yet ascended to the Father" (John 20:17). However, Jesus did not or perhaps could not prevent the women from clasping his feet in a spontaneous act of reverence when he "suddenly" appeared before them after they departed the tomb (Matt. 28:9).

Subsequently, "Jesus appeared in a different form" (Mark 16:12) to two of his followers while they were walking from Jerusalem into the surrounding countryside. "But they were kept from recognizing him" (Luke 24:16) as they traveled on the road to Emmaus, and it was only during supper on that same evening when he broke bread that "their eyes were opened and they recognized him, and he disappeared from their sight" (Luke 24:31).

Then Jesus all of a sudden appeared out of nowhere before the ten or eleven remaining disciples, who were gathered together inside of a locked room where they were staying in Jerusalem (John 20:19). But "they were startled and frightened, thinking they saw a ghost" (Luke 24:37). Jesus reassured them by showing them his wounds and eating a piece of broiled fish (Luke 24:40–43).

Then Jesus appeared "a week later" inside the same locked room and invited doubting St. Thomas to touch his wounds (John 20:26–28). Jesus again appeared to seven disciples on the Sea of Galilee, but at first, "the disciples did not realize that it was Jesus" (John 21:4).

What is going on here? St. Paul provides a plausible explanation by noting the existence of a "spiritual body." He writes, "If there is a natural body, there is also a spiritual body" (1 Cor. 15:44). Paul elsewhere writes that "Jesus Christ … will transform our lowly bodies so that they will be like his glorious body" (Phil. 3:20–21).

The resurrected Jesus resided in his spiritual body, barely apprehensible to our human senses. His form was substantial enough that he could be seen and touched, consume small amounts of food, and speak, but insubstantial enough that he appeared apparition-like. He teetered in and out of this material universe, with one foot on earth and the other in heaven, until he dematerialized completely from this physical realm.

The Sufi mystic Mansur al-Hallaj (858–922) was said to dematerialize and rematerialize at will. Documented reports exist of the late Venezuelan Catholic mystic Maria Esperanza (1928–2004) as having bilocated; this phenomenon has been reported of other Catholic saints, including St. Francis Xavier (1506–1552) and St. Padre Pio (1887–1968). Hinduism also holds that we possess subtle, nonphysical bodies, as does Traditional Chinese Medicine. Those who attain to spiritual illumination may appear to reside in this terrestrial world, but all the while nobody's home. I readily accept that Jesus was an incarnation of God, known in Hinduism as an *avatar*, and as such he interacted with this world from the other side of the fence, as it were, situated on the opposite side from where the rest of us reside. Time and space are mere playthings to such beings.

Now, humans are capable of perceiving a tiny portion of the electromagnetic spectrum known as visible light, which appears from approximately 380 to 700 nanometers.[48] This represents a fractional *0.0035 percent* of the entire electromagnetic spectrum,[49] from dense cosmic rays at the lower end to the longest known wavelengths at the upper end. This means, in practical terms, that we are unable to see 99.9965 percent of what is potentially apprehensible in the universe. Imagine being able to perceive *everything* that takes place around us, if we had but eyes to see.

The human range of hearing is likewise limited to those frequencies between around 20 hertz to 20,000 hertz. We are incapable of hearing infrasound or ultrasound. Yet, audio transmissions occur everywhere constantly, if we had but ears to hear.

Philosopher Gerald Heard notes, "The observational construct (the way we have of instantly seeing the world around as being a series of separate objects) … is not, in point of fact, an accurate picture of what is out there. What is actually out there is an unbroken series of events in a variously accented panorama."[50] In other words, the choppy, partitioned interactions we have with the outer world, which we segregate into a series of separate occurrences, are in fact a singular, continuous occurrence with no distinct points of reference, save our internal sense of "I." But, because our perceptions are screened through the filter of our ego, our "I" occludes this perception. Thus, our ego causes a fragmentizing effect whereby we can't perceive reality as it actually exists. Yet, all the while, we are forever perched on the edge of Infinity.

Our ego serves a purposeful relational function, helping us to distinguish "this" from "that." This partitioning effect is useful for coping with the material world, but it proves a severe handicap when peeling back the artifice of three-dimensional "reality" to encounter God's unembellished form.

When Jesus appeared from Easter Sunday on, he vibrated at a frequency that is outside our myopic sensory perceptions. He anchored himself as best he could in this infinitesimal slice of reality known as earth for as long as he could. But, as if being swept into the vortex of a black hole—a metaphor for the limitless God—his eternal, ethereal form finally lost its tenuous hold on this side of temporal reality, and away he went!

These conjectures, hypothetical as they may seem, nonetheless hold out a distinct hope for devotees of Jesus. If we could but attune ourselves to the same frequency as Jesus, then it is possible that the spiritual form of Jesus—St. Paul's "spiritual body"—into which Jesus transmuted on Easter Sunday, may be apprehended. However, this perception does not occur with our physical eyes and ears but through a direct soul-to-Soul communion, as has been reported by numerous accomplished Christian mystics. St. Peter also said, "God raised him from the dead on the third day and caused him to be seen. He was not seen by all the people, but by witnesses whom God had already chosen ..." (Acts 10:40–41). Thus, Jesus could not—and still cannot—be seen by the vast majority of mortals.

The ability to perceive the spiritual form of Jesus requires us to undergo a radical inner transformation so our soul will attain to an elevated spiritual level we cannot now conceive. In so doing, we leave behind our limited ego and rend asunder the time–space fabric to behold the living God, either as a formless Being, or in the form of Jesus, or in whichever spiritual form most resonates with our soul. Once we cleanse our inner vision, this experience is only a heartbeat away. "For now we see through a glass, darkly; but then we shall see face to face" (1 Cor. 13:12).

Heart to Heart
Website post: May 25, 2023

WHEN WALKING THE SPIRITUAL PATH, it can prove beneficial to step aside from the dualistic rut in which we continually find ourselves and have a frank heart-to-heart talk with our soul, our spiritual self, every now and then. Forget the social pleasantries. Our spiritual welfare is at stake, and we should never kowtow to decorum simply to placate a version of reality that is inherently designed to prevent our spiritual liberation.

Let's face it, we are constantly bombarded with the billboards and Klieg lights of duality, which ensnare us into believing that the sweeping three-dimensional landscape around us is real. Everybody buys into the same deception. Everyone and everything around us continually reinforce this dualistic narrative. We must remember that what we apprehend is merely a construct designed to enact our destiny as it plays itself out in time and space. The idea that we are embodied physical forms bound by gravity to a planet we've made more or less habitable for our species (until now) is, from a

81

nondualistic perspective, utter nonsense. This earthly dimension is merely the illusory platform on which the seeming drama of our lives plays out.

We think we are so-and-so, working at a job, driving a car, living in a home, and so on. We've bought into this fabrication because we—our relative, secular self—are conditioned on a moment-by-moment basis each day to accept this narrow version of "reality." Because of constant societal reinforcement, we are locked into a 24/7 version of reality that severely constricts, if not strangulates, our spiritual self.

Yet, our spiritual self is just the opposite: unbounded, undefined, not tethered to linear time, unshackled by three-dimensional space. It passively, detachedly witnesses as our relative, secular self goes through the motions of life, all the while very much attached. It readily sees through the facade of this universe. But there is typically a massive disconnect between our two selves.

We need to realize that our relative self is merely an actor in a karmic movie that is playing itself out in a material medium, that is, the world around us. We falsely identify with this actor and also with the movie. We interact with various players we perceive in the film, and we have a vested interest in its outcome. We take all this as real. But, through diligent and dedicated spiritual practice—yes, *practice*—we can slowly begin to extract ourselves from this illusion. Once we are able to detach our spiritual self from the boxed-in confines that our secular self occupies, we can actually begin to discern the immense, interconnected web of illusion that envelopes and successfully ensnares perhaps more than 99.9% of humankind.

So, we must frankly ask ourselves: Why do we choose to remain entrapped? Indeed, it is safer to compromise with the status quo and far easier to continue placating to the mass illusion that blankets all with its fog-like veil. Breaking free means stepping apart from the common dualistic denominator in order to walk the spiritual path in earnest. But this does not mean shackling oneself to dogma or rituals or other external accoutrements of religion, which can be equally binding. It does mean delving into the very heart of religion—its mystical element, which is found at the marrow of all religions. This is the source of the vibrant spring where all spirituality originates and flows.

Remember, our spiritual self has nothing to do with any of this. Unlimited in scope and ever free, our spiritual self, as it were, patiently awaits the day when we wake up from our sleepy illusion and reconnect with it. On that day, when we find our lost soul—when the prodigal son or daughter returns home—we completely disengage from this apparition of duality and walk away from the illusory movie in which we find ourselves. The movie can now play itself out, but no longer with our full-scale, all-in participation and involvement. This film is someone else's drama; the actor is not us—we will have shed that role and emerged from our dualistic cocoon to assume our true identity: our eternal spiritual self.

Note to (secular) self: Heart to heart, our spiritual liberation is all that matters.

Jesus of Nazareth: Love's Pure Light

Excerpt from website post: December 25, 2021

Today, Christmas Day, "a Savior has been born." The Babe in the lowly manger would affect humanity like no other. Jesus was in essence pure, radiant love. He lived this love; he taught this love. There are no limits to this love; there are no conditions, no circumstances where this love cannot exist. We seek to realize this same love in our hearts.

The love that Jesus lived and taught is entirely selfless. This love is so powerful it scrapes away the negative accretions of life that have amassed on our soul. It cuts through the accumulated mental debris that obscures our perception of our own spiritual essence. It soothes all the inflammatory emotions that otherwise harm us and others.

This love is not ordinary human love; it is a pure, limitless uncommon spiritual love known as *agapē*—the unconditional, unrestricted, universal love of the unguarded, innocent soul. Through the grace of God and our own diligent spiritual efforts, this overwhelming love can be felt in our heart and manifested in our life.

And so today, divine love became incarnate, the "Word of the Father, now in flesh appearing," as the lyric from *O Come, All Ye Faithful* attests. It is up to us to realize the essence of this pure love in the core of our being. May this selfless love incarnate each day in our hearts, our souls, and in our lives.

Our Shadow Self

Website post: July 22, 2023

FAMED PSYCHOLOGIST CARL G. JUNG (1875–1961) wrote about one's shadow self. In a nutshell, the shadow is composed of all the elements in one's personality that lay dormant in one's unconscious mind. These elements consist of the underlying complexes, hidden drives, unresolved issues, and deep-seated emotional forces that shape our conscious mind and motivate our behavior.

In one sense, our entire spiritual journey could be described as draining the shadow of its vast influence over our lives, our thoughts and words, and our behavior. How often are we driven to do or say things that contradict what we believe? This occurs when our unchecked shadow rules the roost.

For example, we want to love, but we hate. We want to give, but we take. We want to make friends, but we make enemies. Conversely, many times noble, altruistic qualities overtake us, and we embody saintly characteristics that surprise even ourselves. Both positive and negative qualities lurk in one's shadow.

These deeply ingrained traits tend to dominate our personality and cause us to think and act the way we do. The shadow's enormous influence is difficult to rein in because we can't readily put our finger on it. It is as elusive as ... a shadow.

I'm not among those who advocate embracing the shadow, integrating it, honoring it, and so forth. This is tantamount to placating it. By so doing, our shadow rules us, not vice versa. For spiritual aspirants, the goal is to deplete the shadow's power over us and thereby overcome its stealth but considerable influence in our lives. If we can accomplish this, our thought patterns and behavior will change.

Rather than spending years in therapy attempting to untangle ourselves from the grip of our shadow, which is the modern Western method to attain individuation (i.e., psychological maturation and emotional stability), some ancient Eastern methods go right to the source by decisively cutting it off. We consequently attain freedom from its effects, both good and bad. One such method is found in the Vedic sage Patanjali's Yogasūtra, which disregards the *contents* of the shadow (which are stored in one's *chitta,* or mind), and simply says that liberation is attained when *all* mental vacillations cease (Yogasūtra 1:2).

What a refreshing idea! Instead of spending hours sifting through one's mental landscape and micro-analyzing its contents—especially negative elements—with some overpaid therapist, simply transcend those contents by bringing their functioning to an abrupt halt. If many notable Western psychologists had studied Patanjali, and if they had far less ego, they could have spared the world reams of useless theory by cutting to the chase and liberating people instead of analyzing all their inner debris and providing them with superficial palliative coping mechanisms.

However, this is no doubt easier said than done. When walking the spiritual path, we are attempting to extract ourselves from the Pandora's box of hidden motivations and kneejerk emotions that affect us around the clock. To gain the upper hand, we need to practice spiritual disciplines on a routine basis.

Some of the most effective practices involve concentrating the mind until it becomes totally focused on and absorbed in one object alone, which shuts down the mind. These practices can be found in the major religions, including Catholicism (Contemplative Prayer), Theravada Buddhism (the "Contemplation" sections of the Noble Eightfold Path), and of course Patañjali's Yogasūtra from Hinduism. Concentration lifts our awareness above the turbulent waves of our unruly lower mind. Our awareness then increasingly adheres to our spiritual self, which is unaffected by such vicissitudes.

With continued practice, the impact of the unconscious influences residing within us is reduced. What emerges are our higher, spiritual qualities. We come to embody feelings of love, joy, profound inner peace, and a giving heart. The light that radiates from our luminous soul is far greater than the darkness cast by our shadow. We come to live in the radiance of this spiritual light, which is the ultimate remedy to counteract and transcend our shadow self.

Pattern of Prestige

Excerpt from website post: June 21, 2023

The real solution to the pervasive lack of civility and common courtesy, combined with the thorough routing of ethical standards we often see around us, is—as the 1955 song reminds us—"Let There Be Peace on Earth, and Let It Begin with Me." We may become justifiably upset when some shopper aggressively races to beat us to the checkout counter at our local supermarket, but it is imperative we do not replicate their antagonistic behavior and get into an incident. We may be victimized by theft, and while it's morally imperative to condemn the actions of and, if possible, seek legal reparations from the perpetrators, we do not stoop to this level of behavior ourselves. By not allowing ourselves to take on these unacceptable qualities and by de-escalating potentially volatile situations, we effectively stop their spread. And, by not taking the next step and retaliating, we rise above the endemic pervasiveness of these aberrant behaviors and become a pattern of prestige ourselves, a living role model, which in turn is modeled on the principles of civility and courtesy that are inherent in the ethical injunctions enjoined by all the great religions. In so doing, the example set by one lone person becomes a beacon to others, one small candle at a time.

Do Not Lose Your Inner Peace
Website post: August 12, 2023

MANY ARE FAMILIAR WITH St. Teresa of Ávila's (1515–1582, Spain) well-known Bookmark prayer:

> *Let nothing disturb you,*
> *Let nothing cause you fear.*
> *Everything passes away;*
> *God alone never changes.*
> *Patience obtains all things.*
> *Whoever has God lacks nothing;*
> *God alone suffices.*[51]

St. Francis de Sales (1567–1622, France) had a similar saying:

> *Never be in a hurry;*
> *Do everything quietly*
> *And in a calm spirit.*

> *Do not lose your inner peace*
> *For anything whatsoever,*
> *Even if your whole world seems upset.*[52]

Both these Catholic saints convey a profound message. This idea can readily be traced to Jesus' counsel: "Do not worry about your life" (Matt. 6:25).

One's entire spiritual life could revolve around these sayings.

Looking at Francis' precept "Do not lose your inner peace for anything whatsoever" in greater depth, we could glibly observe that in today's manic world, this sounds like a good idea in theory but is not attainable in practice. From dawn to dusk, many circumstances seemingly conspire to trigger us to lose our inner poise. Yet, all such circumstances have two things in common: (1) they are caused by outer events; or (2) they are caused by our own emotional reactions. Sometimes they are caused by a combination of the two. (In fact, it is our emotional reactions to *any* event that are the real culprits.)

Outer events that set us off could be anything, such as getting stuck in traffic on the way to an important meeting, thus making us late. Or a hacker stealing our Social Security number. Our child breaks their leg falling off a swing. A neighbor's errant weed-whacking throws a stone that cracks our windshield. The situations are endless. Pressures, deadlines, delays. Problems created by others, problems created by ourselves. Unexpected turns of events, thwartings, obstacles, losses. We get whipsawed by forces outside our control, and we lose our cool.

In addressing the myriad of outer triggers, I'll cite an apt section from my spiritual novel, *Dialogues With the Lord of Time*, "When a person's peace of mind is so easily swayed by external events, it indicates they have little faith. Faith is the inner experience that keeps one spiritually grounded regardless of the impact of any external circumstance. An advanced aspirant's mind will remain unmoved by fortune or misfortune, justice or injustice, blessings or travails."[53]

So, what is the solution? Unshakable faith in our spiritual essence; unshakable faith in the object of our worship (for example, Jesus, Allah, Buddha, Tara, Krishna); unshakable faith in God; unshakable faith in an ultimate reality—whichever resonates with us spiritually. This is the antidote to losing our inner poise.

The very next paragraph in *Dialogues* addresses our tempestuous emotional reactions that jostle us inwardly: "When your mind turns inward and becomes firmly rooted by faith in the spiritual core of your being, you will no longer react to external events, be they 'good' or 'bad.' This is the true test of spiritual progress: making the mind turn inward until it becomes so deeply anchored in the fertile spiritual soil within that it will not react at any time to anything."[54]

So again, the answer for us is to possess a deep, unwavering faith. This helps immunize us from reacting emotionally both to outer events and to the ongoing parade of thoughts, emotions, and images that float through our minds. Okay, then, how do we cultivate such faith?

Through effort, determination, and resolve. We make an unswerving inner commitment that, *No matter what, I will adhere to my act of faith, and nothing but nothing will shake me, deter me, or drag me away from my conviction.*

We initially take small steps. We may stumble at first; if so, we try again. Every time we are successful, this reinforces our resolve. Soon, over time, we gain confidence in our practice. Every time we do not allow outer events to push our buttons; every time we do not react emotionally, we gain proficiency in our practice. Eventually, we gain mastery. It is entirely possible for us to realize and embody St. Francis de Sales' wise maxim at all times in our lives: "Do not lose your inner peace for anything whatsoever."

Meditation – Benefits and Beyond
Excerpt from website post: December 10, 2022

Beyond the physical benefits that meditation imparts, there are more profound upsides. The practice of meditation is one of the gateways to access one's spiritual self. Now, those who engage in mindfulness meditation might cringe at the thought of associating their practice with anything that smacks of religion. But, call it what you will—we're calling it one's spiritual self—there is a deeper aspect within us that lies beyond our worldly personality. This inner component can be accessed through meditation and, over time, with continued practice, one can maintain a connection with one's spiritual self during activity. Or, to rephrase this idea without using religious terminology, one can maintain the same state of mindfulness that is achieved when meditating while engaged in activity.

Focusing the mind for protracted periods of time invariably brings about a state of concentration. The ability to concentrate may be alien to the emerging TikTok generation, which relies on constant commotion to make an impact. But prolonged concentration leads to what is formally called *dhyāna* (meditation) in the ancient Vedic seer Patanjali's manual of liberation, the Yogasūtra. This is an uninterrupted, undisturbed state of focused mental quiescence, absent all thoughts, mental images, and emotional sensations. Repeatedly attaining this state through regular practice opens the door to accessing several increasingly progressive degrees of *samadhi*—abstract states of deep inner absorption. The keyword here is practice—regular practice—and by such practice the true value of meditation can unfold within us, which is its ability to confer spiritual illumination. According to those mystics who have attained this ultimate state, no words can describe it. This is the priceless feature of meditation that can't be measured, and this immeasurable benefit can be attained by all.

The Unquenchable Fire Within

Previously unpublished essay: May 2021[55]

Come, my sweet Beloved!
Burn my reins with Thy fire
Then take Thine heat and kindle my whole heart
Ignite and illumine my very soul
With the bliss of Thy sweet love
And destroy all things that would take
My mind or body from Thee![56]

–Richard Rolle

WHEN THE GREEK GOD PROMETHEUS defied Zeus by stealing fire and bringing it to the human race, he unwittingly unleashed a force that has both aided and harmed humankind ever since. As we mortals very soon discovered, fire indeed has two aspects: constructive and benign; and destructive, often malevolent. We witness the positive effects of fire as exemplified by the sun's warmth, which gives life to earth's creatures, plants, and ocean organisms. We warm our homes, cook our food, and sometimes utilize fire for light. But fire can also prove harmful, as when a house fire destroys a residence, or an uncontrollable wildfire rages through communities, leaving a wake of destruction and, at times, a devastating death toll in its path.

Yet this dual nature of fire parallels the dual nature of life itself. Every yin has its yang. The positive and negative aspects of fire are two facets of the same phenomenon. From fire's destruction comes renewal, as when natural forest fires help to restore ecological homeostasis by regenerating the affected terrain, thus rendering it capable of sustaining new life. Fire's favorable–unfavorable dimension is personified in one manifestation of Agni, the Hindu god of fire, which is depicted as having two faces, symbolizing these same dual aspects.

When we are confronted with fire's destructive power—such as escaping a volcanic eruption or evacuating from a wildfire—many times we are called upon to practice nobler qualities of character: endurance, to handle hardship amid adversity; trust, to have faith in the unknown; frugality, to do without routine conveniences; and adaptability, to be flexible during times of crisis. When things go well, anyone can appear saintly. But when our world is turned upside down, our character is put to the test by demonstrating how well we manage during the upheaval. The challenges we face compel us to tap into and utilize our higher character traits. Our inner nature is forged by such adversities. So again, we see how fire's destructive aspect can produce a constructive outcome, which in this case affects us by positively reshaping our character.

In Traditional Chinese Medicine (TCM), fire is one of five elements that must maintain a balanced interrelationship with the other four elements in order for harmony to prevail. On a planetary scale, this elemental balance has been disrupted by unchecked carbon emissions, triggering an unprecedented change in earth's climate as indicated by widespread global-warming patterns, which may be teetering past the point of no return. But this same process finds a parallel on a microcosmic scale. Within humans, the element of fire must exist in harmony with all other elements—wood, earth, air, and water—or the result is imbalance, which can manifest as various psychological disorders and physical illnesses.

However, in the innermost realm of our being, whether one chooses to call it a soul or, as in Buddhism, if one declares there is no soul (*anattā*), there nonetheless exists a core, an inner spiritual essence that is neither physical nor psychological. Traditional religions assert that this spiritual core is our true nature. And many technologies exist to aid us in connecting with our spiritual essence. But to perceive our spiritual nature, do we acquire something we presently lack, or do we shed that which we don't actually own? The answer depends on how we define our self.

While each of us possesses fundamental traits that define our personality, our personality itself is in a constant state of flux, buffeted and affected at every turn by reactive emotions, ingrained behaviors, persistent memories, and an often-intractable ego, which occasionally leads us by the nose into detrimental predicaments. We must transcend this relative self in order to catch a glimpse of our true spiritual nature. When we make productive efforts that loosen the layers which envelop us and prevent us from perceiving and identifying with our radiant inner essence, we access new levels of awareness within us.

And so, we now have our answer. As we divest ourselves of our mental detritus, we *simultaneously* attain to more refined planes of awareness, ones with fewer psychological and emotional accoutrements. To paraphrase the Bengali saint Sri Ramakrishna: If you peel off an onion's outer red skin, then continue peeling the thick inner white skins, you'll find nothing at the core. Likewise, if the ego is analyzed, it will be found to have no real substance.[57] As we peel off the layers of our personality and ego, we discover that nothing but unadorned consciousness is present at the core of our beings.

One element that can help propel us toward a rendezvous with our pure consciousness within is fire. References to fire and the heat it radiates are found in mystical literature both symbolically and literally. For example, some aspirants have attested to palpable sensations of inner warmth that are generated during the course of their practices. However, we will primarily employ fire's figurative usages in our present discussion. Thus we can state that, once stirred, this internal fire burns through the layers encrusting our spiritual nature. On all levels, as it advances straight to the inmost core of our being, it incinerates the barriers that prevent us from perceiving our effulgent essence. When we're consumed by the raging flames of inner purification, we can see that multiple psychological obscurations, emotional blockages, and similar unconscious points of congestion are set ablaze along its unstoppable path.

This inner fiery force is known in Vedic religion as *tapas*—"to burn"—which Sanskrit scholar Judith M. Tyberg, Ph.D. (1902–1980), explained, in the context of applied spirituality, is "a burning, flaming devotion to the attaining of the spiritual goal."[58] Tapas is ignited by inner yearning and stoked by continual, dedicated practice. As it spreads, it targets the invisible yet very tangible cords that bind our spiritual nature to the confines of duality. Our spiritual aspirations must be more powerful than both our present mindsets and our deep-seated habit patterns. In fact, many elements of our fluctuating personality are nothing more than repetitious habit patterns that are continually reenacted and continuously reinforced. Intense inner fire is needed to burn through these layers of deeply ingrained habitual responses and kneejerk emotional reactions to reveal our incandescent spiritual core within.

Generating and sustaining this tapas is a prerequisite of spiritual unfoldment. By doing so, we ignite the symbolic flame inside us—the "fire of love," the "living flame of love," as mystically described by English hermit Richard Rolle (ca. 1300–1349) and St. John of the Cross (1542–1591), respectively. This fire then burns through the many sheaths of illusion that enshroud our spiritual nature. Heat is a product of friction, and this friction, or vibration, provides the propulsion necessary to advance us on our spiritual journey. Vibration is the underlying condition of the universe, as represented by the eternal ecstatic embrace of Shiva and Parvati, and as discerned as the resonating, pulsating *pranava* (OM) that underscores all creation.[59] Our intense desire for enlightenment creates this friction inside us. During our undaunted spiritual efforts, we utilize this blistering vibratory thermal momentum to drive us ever onward toward our goal.

As we generate tapas through our one-pointed focus, which is aimed at accessing our spiritual core, many inner purifications take place. The most important of these are known in classic yogic schools as purification of the mind (*chitta-shuddhi*) and purification of the circulatory system within our subtle bodies (*nadi-shuddhi*).

(*Nadis* are synonymous with meridians in TCM.) These twin purifications cleanse our minds and, equally important, purify our subtle bodies by making them capable of sustaining the higher states of realization while we inhabit our physical bodies.

Mental purification consists of rewiring our inner psychological architecture by dislodging the negative components (e.g., unruly emotional reactions, unproductive personality patterns, undesirable behaviors) within our character that hinder our spiritual progress. Purification of the nadis is best achieved by taking care of our physical body in ways that include appropriate diet, regular exercise, proper rest, and moderation in all things.

It is also critically important to routinely practice deep meditation or other focused spiritual practices that expand the delicate meditative state (*dhyāna*) throughout our denser body–mind infrastructure.[60] This can generate warmth and bring about inner cleansing, similar to a fever burning up an underlying infection. One Hindu spiritual path known as *shaktipat* forcefully awakens the *kundalini*, a powerful spiritual energy said to reside within us. Once awakened, the disciple, in a state of surrender, allows the kundalini to burn up their inner impurities.

In addition, we would never purchase a home with leaky pipes, faulty wiring, or outdated insulation. Similarly, we should never settle for mediocrity in our spiritual life. If we experience bliss or visions or achieve steady inner concentration, these are all positive signposts, but there is always *more* to attain. We cannot even remotely conceive in our present state what the saints and sages describe as enlightenment. All such imaginings fall short of the luminous, living, vibrant experience itself. This is why we must persevere and travel along whichever path we follow in good faith, assured that the multitudinous fruits of realization will crown us in the end. Sri Ramakrishna again provides an apt parable:

> Once a destitute woodcutter eked out a meager living by daily selling a load of wood he had cut in a neighboring forest. One day he met a holy man, who advised him, 'My dear son, go farther.' The woodcutter returned home, wondering why the sage had spoken these words. Some days passed. Then, recalling the holy man's counsel, he made up his mind to go farther into the

forest. Much to his surprise, he came upon an extensive grove of sandalwood trees. He soon brought cartloads of sandalwood to market and grew enormously rich. After a few days, he was once more reminded of the holy man's words, 'Go farther.' The woodcutter ventured even more remotely into the forest and discovered a copper mine. He took with him all the copper he could carry and sold it in the marketplace and acquired even more wealth. The next day, without stopping at the copper mine, he proceeded even farther, as the sage had advised, and he came upon a silver mine near a riverbed. He brought away tons of silver and became even richer. After some time had lapsed, the holy man's words again echoed in his mind. He thought to himself, 'The holy man did not tell me I should stop at the silver mine; he told me to go farther.' This time the wood-cutter crossed the river and spotted a gold mine. He extracted the gold, and his wealth grew beyond his wildest dreams. A few more days passed. Then he said to himself, 'Well, the holy man instructed me to go farther.' So he advanced into an even deeper part of the forest and found a diamond mine, which made him as wealthy as the god of wealth.[61]

Our goal is nothing short of full-blown enlightenment: unbounded and dimensionless; affecting and transcending our body, mind, and emotions; and centering us squarely in our spiritual core. This is a mul-tifaceted realization, which radically alters our worldly selves, aligns us with our innermost consciousness, and from there radiates outward, benignly touching all those with whom we come into contact. Our journey begins with somethingness and ends with nothingness. Yet this nothingness possesses attributes that are apprehensible to humans—unlimited peace; never-ending joy; and unrestricted, causeless love. These same attributes adhere more and more to our relative self over time as our realization unfolds until our relative self is altogether eclipsed by our spiritual self. Our inner spiritual fire helps bring about this all-consuming, transformative realization—a state wherein we experience undifferentiated oneness and inexhaustible, limitless love, as theologically expressed in an ecstatic vision by St. Mary Magdalene de' Pazzi (1566–1607), "I only saw Him love Himself with pure love, recognise [*sic*] Himself in His boundlessness, [and] embrace all things created with pure and boundless love."[62]

It is we who must muster up and utilize our internal flame in order to set fire to the thorny thickets that entrap us in our mortal cages. We were born not to wallow in the muck of earthly travails, nor to amass various superficial adornments for our bodies and egos, but to rise above our terrestrial moorings and soar with the highest class of angels. Yet, we alone keep ourselves bound to the world of finitude. We so readily accept the dualistic worldview, which is imposed on us at every moment, that it becomes second nature. However, it is up to us to awaken from our illusory dream. Instead of living with and pandering to our dualistic mind, we can burn through its constrictive shackles by harnessing the interior conflagration created by our tapas—our intense fiery spiritual efforts. If we but loosen the grip of this illusive sheath that surrounds our spiritual core and peer out from our temporal shell, we shall know true inner freedom.

Our real home is the wondrous, ever-new ethereal realm that lies within our beings, hewn from immortal redwoods, forever resistant to change, and unaffected by all earthly trappings that would deter us from realizing our spiritual vision. There, when situated firmly in our real nature, we are free from time; bathed in a continuous blissful, transcendent joy; and liberated from the deleterious effects of sorrow and the woes of this life. The "unquenchable fire" (Matt. 3:12) within us, having fulfilled its ultimate purpose by rewiring our psychological architecture, purifying our mind and subtle body, subduing our ego, and quelling our reactive emotions, now recedes to a mere ember. Having been fashioned in the crucible of our inner spiritual inferno, we are newly created beings, born afresh to inhabit our true nature in a perpetual state of wonderment and awe. Emerging as if from a chrysalis, we come to perceive and identify with our refulgent spiritual essence, shining in all its radiant splendor. Thus, we are enabled to live a celestial life here on earth—fully alive to our spiritual core, and ever-residing in the boundless heavens within. Thereafter, we are able to breathe the air of the devas and walk among the perennially verdant gardens of the gods, where Prometheus himself may be seen smiling beneficently on us and others who have skillfully and wisely utilized both aspects of his great gift.

Henosis

Excerpt from website post: May 12, 2023

Henosis is the ancient Greek word for mystical union with the ultimate reality. This is no theoretical concept. In his Enneads, Plotinus, who famously said that spiritual life consists of "the flight of the alone to the Alone," outlines different stages the aspirant must undergo to achieve this union. These stages are systematized, quite sophisticated, and well worthy of further study.

We do find parallels, of course, in other religions. This same state is variously described in different traditions, West and East, which demonstrates it is universal. Whenever one human being attains a given spiritual state, then any and all human beings can attain that exact same state. Henosis, *samadhi, nirvāṇa,* or any of these states are not outside us; they exist within us. We can access and increasingly manifest them during the course of our spiritual journey.

Our spiritual goal is to have a direct one-on-one experience with the ultimate reality, which in a theological context is called God. Our soul or spiritual self then becomes enveloped by the living presence of God and subsumed into God's infinitude. During the deepest stages of henosis, the switch that supplies the electrical current to our ego is shut off; the alone then encounters the Alone, freed from all intermediaries, definitions, and points of reference. At that extraordinary stage, which is our birthright, all is one.

The Essence of Sufism
Website post: June 10, 2023

ISLAM IS ONE OF THE WORLD'S great monotheistic religions. It was founded during the seventh century by Muhammad ibn Abdullah (570–632), revered by his followers as a prophet and messenger of God. Its followers are called Muslims, "those who submit," that is, to the will of God or Allah. The root meaning of the word "Islam" in Arabic (اسلام) is *submission*.

The mystical element within Islam is Sufism. The essence of Sufism is exactly the same as Islam: surrender. And so, we need to define what is meant by the parallel terms *surrender* and *submission* in the eyes of Sufis.

But first, there is no such thing as a generic "Sufi." There are many Sufi orders, whose adherents follow lineages that are often named after their founders, similar to Catholic monastics belonging to Benedictine, Dominican, or Franciscan orders. Each Sufi lineage stresses different practices, but they uniformly emphasize total submission to God.

All Sufi orders belong to Islam, although orthodox Islam doesn't always look with favor upon Sufism. We won't discuss this issue in our present essay, but we will turn our attention to the concept and practice of surrender.

When we encounter people and situations in our day-to-day lives, we view some as favorable and some as unfavorable. A surrendered Sufi doesn't have this divisive mindset. *All* is seen as God or Allah to them. We look on certain people as vexatious and certain circumstances in our lives as obstacles to be overcome. A true Sufi who has submitted themselves to God has neither enemies nor obstacles, but views all things as inherently infused with God, as originating from God, as leading to God, as part of God. A mystical rendering of the great Islamic Pillar of Faith, the *Shahadah* ("La ilaha ill'Allah"), is "There is nothing but God."

This concept is hard for us to imagine. A Sufi mystic looks at life not as we view life, but from the other side. They strive to overcome their *nafs*, or ego, and this requires a radical inner shift brought about by entirely reorienting their perspective from their ego to God. They drain their self of its noisy demands, and they forfeit their personal wants and desires, and as a result they attain instant peace. They merge their will with God's will, so that—*poof!*—their ego vanishes, and only one Will remains.

As Abdul–Qadir al–Jilani (1078–1166), the Sufi master after whom the Qadiri Sufi Order is named, observed, "In reality there is no doer of anything excepting God."[63] To an illumined Sufi, this is no theory. They come to *live* these words through their personal experience. Having relinquished their self-will, a Sufi possesses unshakable trust in God, and they are forever unruffled by the tumult of this world. They feel an enduring inner calmness, and they maintain equanimity under all circumstances. Thus, they are never perturbed, anxious, worried, or fearful. They have realized the essence of Sufism by abiding continuously in a state of complete surrender at all times.

We can benefit our own spiritual lives by establishing within us a deep-seated attitude of trust, joyous surrender, and self-effacing submission that effectively anchors us in our spiritual core. These qualities help guide us every moment. They immunize us from the ups and downs we experience throughout life.

The Eight Fetters, Pt. I
Website post: October 12, 2023

IN THE *GOSPEL OF SRI RAMAKRISHNA*, the well-known Hindu spiritual teacher Ramakrishna (1836–1886) frequently mentions the "eight fetters." The eight fetters, or *aṣṭapaśas*, are as follows: shame, hatred, fear, pride of class, pride of upbringing, pride of good character, grief, and doubt. We will examine each of the eight fetters in this and my next post. I should note that Buddhism has its own lists of fetters, such as belief in a permanent self, attachment to rituals, and so forth, which are equally worthy of examination. But our focus today is on the Hindu compilation.

Shame: We do something that causes us embarrassment or disgrace, then we feel humiliated. Actually, this humbling experience is a positive response, essential for curbing our ego and retraining ourselves to embrace more productive behavior patterns. However, if we wallow in feelings of shame, this can create a sticking point in our character. If we have acted badly or in a hurtful manner, we should indeed express remorse and apologize as necessary and also change our ways, but we should not wear our sense of shame around our necks like a millstone. Make amends, and don't repeat the objectionable behavior. Chalk it up to a learning experience, then move on.

Hatred: Hatred is feeling strong aversion toward something or animosity toward someone or a group of people. Feelings of hatred should obviously be avoided. However, there is nothing wrong, in my opinion, for not particularly *liking* someone or something, or not wanting to chum up to them. A person doesn't necessarily have to like their overbearing boss; we aren't required to befriend our kid's archrival soccer team or invite a burglar over for afternoon tea. Just make sure you remain as indifferent as possible.

Sometimes we feel a strong resistance toward performing tedious tasks, such as packaging a defective item for return to an online seller, or placing that fifth follow-up phone call to our utility company to find out when our electricity will be restored following an outage. But when our aversions turn into a visceral, kneejerk outpouring of negative, vitriolic feelings toward another or toward something, we are caught up in hatred. Hatred is like a festering wound that won't heal. We must be more neutral toward nettlesome people and trying situations that we find bothersome, but without crossing that fine line and triggering a response of hatred within us.

Fear: Fear can produce crippling effects in our lives. Repeated feelings of fear or ongoing exposure to a fear- or anxiety-producing situation can cause PTSD, which is difficult to overcome because it overstimulates and can even affect the functioning of the brain's amygdala, which can create a vicious circle of heightened anxiety-related responses. We can overcome certain fears and anxieties through dedicated training. However, if fearfulness is severe and persistent, then seeking competent medical treatment can be a viable option. The goal is to free ourselves from fears while prudently retaining a cautionary approach as warranted when navigating the byways of our daily lives.

Also, it should be noted that some nutritionists believe our intake of certain foods and foodstuffs like sugar or overly processed food artifacts can alter one's mood, as can nutritional deficiencies. There are various theories of foods and their effects on humans in India (Ayurveda) and China (Traditional Chinese Medicine or TCM), which are worth investigating. According to Ayurveda, eating excessive amounts of certain *rajasic* foods—for example, various hot spices—can stimulate irritability or aggression. Other foods that are classified according to TCM as *yin*—such as certain fruits and raw vegetables—can induce anxiety if overconsumed. The ideal is to find food combinations that agree with one's constitution and one's biochemical individuality, and which are nourishing and produce balance, resulting in a healthy body and calm state of mind.

Pride of Class: We are born in an upper-middle-class household. We feel superior to those who are situated in a lower social stratum than ours. Well, the cure is to look no further than those who are wealthier than us, which will readily deflate any pride we feel. But, counterproductively, this can also produce envy: "Ah, if I were only as rich as that Powerball jackpot winner who just bought a mansion in Malibu." The remedy is, as Ralph Waldo Emerson (1803–1882) wisely mused, "There is a time in every man's education when he arrives at the conviction that envy is ignorance; that imitation is suicide; that he must take himself for better, for worse, as his portion …"[64]

The Eight Fetters, Pt. II
Website post: October 25, 2023

THIS CONCLUDES OUR EXAMINATION of what are known in Hinduism as the eight fetters. Today, we will review the last four of these fetters.

Pride of Upbringing: We come from a lineage of important persons with pedigreed ancestry. We were educated at an elitist university. We mingle with well-to-do, cultured peers. We live in a custom-crafted home. We never shop at Walmart or eat at Denny's. We think, "Thank God we are affluent and can live far more civilized lives than the hoi polloi who live on the other side of the tracks." Well, once this thought crosses your mind, you behave far worse than the so-called hoi polloi, who may in fact be morally superior to you because they lack your haughtiness. If you embody all the graces and manners inherent in gentility, but if you are an arrogant snob, such overweening pride may be your spiritual downfall. Don't even think of wearing your upbringing as a badge of honor. Your snobbishness will impede whatever spiritual progress you hope to achieve. Jesus dined with sinners and tax-collectors (the latter of which were reviled in Jesus' day, and it appears, by and large, they still are today). Get off your high horse and strip yourself of your nonsensical pretenses.

Pride of Good Character: We don't steal, we don't murder, we don't slander, we don't lie, we don't cheat on our spouse. Great. But if you pride yourself on your good conduct, your very pride may lead to your spiritual ruin. "Pride goeth before ... a fall" (Prov. 16:18). It's imprudent to flaunt any supposed holier-than-thou achievements in public; such actions could come back to bite you. Jesus cautions (Matt. 6:5–6) against parading your spirituality before others, as do other spiritual teachers. The cure: humble yourself and approach each day as though you are a novice on the spiritual path.

Grief: There are major events in our lives that cause tremendous sadness: the death of a loved one or a beloved pet; the loss of a job; a permanent medical injury. The list is endless. Buddha created a whole philosophy of life based on *dukkha*—the frustrations, sufferings, and losses of life. If we allow grief to overwhelm us, it will paralyze us. If we wallow in sadness, we will have ceased to move ahead in life. Grieve as necessary—some losses can never be overcome, so we can never be expected to "get over" them. But move forward on the road of life—the clock is ticking, and it's up to us to come to terms with our losses and sorrows, while not allowing them to overtake and cripple us.

Doubt: Maintaining a healthy skepticism can be a valuable ally in today's world of scammers, con artists, and hackers. But when this becomes an ingrained trait, it can border on catastrophic thinking. This kind of predisposed negative outlook can color our entire attitude. In a spiritual context, doubt can kill one's faith as well as one's enthusiasm for practice. Some practical tips: avoid negative people—those who drag you down, and, as singer Diana Ross once said, those who "[void liquid waste] on your dreams."[65] Don't listen to those who instill doubt in you. Such people are toxic and serve no purpose in our lives. In addition, try not to allow self-doubt to take hold. Be positive, upbeat, and optimistic, and do not allow the trials, travails, and defeats of this world to beat you down. Once your self-confidence is shaken, or worse, destroyed, much time and effort is often required to restore it. So, never allow doubt to take hold. And never give up.

One more: I don't have a name for this. But there is an undercurrent of a certain harshness, self-centeredness, meanness, ruthlessness, callousness, and cynicism; a reveling in the superficial and the trivial; the shameless worship of money and blind adoration of self-indulgent luxury; and a rampant maliciousness, often teetering into blatant *schadenfreude*—all of which collectively run rampant through certain segments of our present American society. Perhaps aided and abetted by certain mainstream media pot-stirrers and social-media "influencers," this wholly negative sentiment erodes any sense of community and commonality, goodwill and empathy that should serve as a primary ethical cornerstone of a flourishing society. Spiritual aspirants must not succumb to this aberrant, regressive mindset.

Along these lines, a BBC article from last summer, commenting on the fall of a British politician, wrote of the larger "fundamental pillars" of society: "Conduct. Behaviour. Believability. Integrity. The sanctity of truth. The contempt for lies."[66] Oh, how true.

A twofold remedy to counteract the influence of this pernicious social disease is to practice compassion and to maintain our own ethical code regardless of circumstances. This helps to shield ourselves against these malignant influences. According to Hindu belief, this age is known as Kali Yuga—a dark age where only 25% of spirituality flourishes. Thus, we can expect this exact kind of widespread uptick in brazen materialism, unprincipled self-indulgence, the mindless adulation of secularism, and role models often personified by those who lack both a steady moral compass and any smidgen of concern for others. If we are affected by this nameless syndrome or in any way get caught up in its downward-spiraling effects, we can easily lose sight of our spiritual goal, and therefore this constitutes a fetter.

In conclusion, succumbing to any of these eight—nine—fetters can hinder and create impediments on our spiritual path, which will bring our spiritual progress to a crashing halt. However, we can overcome them first by recognizing them, then by practicing single-minded determination to center our awareness in our spiritual self at all times. We can thereby, through conviction and persistence, resist the insidious influence of these and all fetters by keeping our mind undeviatingly fixed on our spiritual goal.

Ecstatic Utterances from Mount Sinai

Previously unpublished writing: July 2009 (source) and March 2024

"Hear O Israel the Lord our God, the Lord is One" (Deut. 6:4). Moses' powerful declaration signaled the beginning of monotheistic Judaism. The one Jewish God is viewed as both transcendent and immanent—beyond the universe and within it, both impersonal and personal.

"Love the Lord your God with all your heart, and with all your soul, and with all your mind, and with all your strength" (Deut. 6:5). With this second pronouncement, Moses commandingly conveyed the additional quintessential element of Judaism, which is how we humans should interact with the one God: *love God above all things*. When these two scriptural passages from the Torah are conjoined, the resultant two-prong approach is all the Jewish mystics needed. According to them, God can be experienced, and many dove head-long into this divine calling by undertaking practices so they could know God firsthand.

The Hasidic and other Jewish mystical and meditational movements of recent centuries emphasize that the devotee must develop and maintain a deep, loving relationship with God. They frequently employ *devekut*—the practice of cleaving to God—to achieve this goal. There are formal techniques as well, such as *Hisbonenus* meditation. With the advent of the Jewish Renewal Movement in the late twentieth century, an abundance of these practices have become widely available.

When studying under a capable rabbi and receiving the blessings of their lineage, a portal can be opened whereby a palpable wellspring of the ancient Jewish mystical current is released and tangibly engulfs the student's inner being. When performing *mitzvas*, the diligent Jewish practitioner joyfully gives back to the creation. They wholeheartedly love God and demonstrate this love by loving God's creation. The circuit is now complete. Humans are the conduits that facilitate this loop of endless love reverberating throughout the cosmos. These ecstatic utterances from Mount Sinai echo today in the hearts and souls and minds of devout contemporary Jewish mystics, who are driven by divine love and motivated by sheer joy to tap into the underlying essence of manifest and unmanifest creation, which is the one, undivided God, *Hashem*, with whom they endlessly dance in inner ecstasy.

Aggregates and Qualities
Website post: October 22, 2022

IN BUDDHISM, A KEY TERM IS *SKANDHA*, which translates as "aggregate." This refers to the five components of one's being as defined in Buddhist thought: one's material form (i.e., our body), sensations, perceptions, mental activity, and consciousness.

A similar concept exists in Hinduism, originating from the Sankhya philosophical school, which advances the principle of the *gunas* ("qualities"). All things are said to be composed of three gunas: *sattva* (equilibrium or balance), *rajas* (activity or motion), and *tamas* (stasis or inertia). These qualities apply both macrocosmically and microcosmically, that is, to the universe at large, and, paralleling the Buddhist skandhas, to one's psychophysical form.

Aggregates and qualities are considered universal constants. Their common feature is *change*. They are ephemeral, ever-mutable elements or processes existing in time and space. They are external to the underlying ultimate reality and our unchanging spiritual self.

And therein lies a massive misunderstanding.

One of Buddhism's foundational tenets postulates that there is "no self" (*anattā*), which is traditionally used to argue against what Buddhists characterize as the Hindu doctrine of a permanent self. However, I agree with the late Professor Jay Lakhani's insightful analysis: there has been a longstanding misinterpretation of Buddha's teaching on this subject.[67] Buddha did not deny the spiritual or immaterial essence of a person (technically, *paramatman*) but rather one's transitory, impermanent self or ego (technically, *jivatman*). Over the centuries, this distinction became blurred, and the word *jivatman* was shortened simply, and mistakenly, to *atman*, termed *attā* in Buddhism. Scholars such as Ananda Coomaraswamy and Kamaleswar Bhattacharya also support this view. Buddhists refer to the immaterial essence within and outside us as *emptiness*. For Buddhists to continue mistaking the word *atman* for *jivatman* does a disservice both to Hindus and to the Buddha himself.

On a universal level, Hindus refer to the omnipresent spiritual reality as *Brahman*. Jewish mystics call it *Hashem*; Christians, *God* or *Heavenly Father*; Islamic practitioners, *Allah*; Taoists, *Tao* or "The Way." These are simply names denoting the infinite spiritual reality as opposed to the temporal reality. For humans, there must always be a name for that which is Nameless.

Our interactions with this physical world are viewed in Buddhism as merely aggregates interacting with aggregates. The Dalai Lama distills the essence of this concept as it applies to a person: "Neither am I the body nor the aggregates."[68] Similarly, Krishna states in the Bhagavad Gita, per my liberal rendition, "In reality, all activity occurs because of the continual interactions of changing material processes (gunas). It is only when a person mistakenly affixes the sensation of 'I' (*ahankara*) on to these changing material processes that they become deluded into thinking that it is they who perform actions" (Gita 3:27).

Beyond the aggregates of Buddhism and the qualities of Hinduism lies the ultimate reality, which we find within ourselves. This is our spiritual self, our inherent nature: infinite, ever-blissful, peaceful beyond words. Along with focusing on attaining our spiritual goal, our primary spiritual tasks while sojourning on earth are to stop identifying with the aggregates and to transcend all qualities. Thereby, we can realize our true immutable spiritual nature.

The Ultimate Healing
Website post: March 12, 2022

THE ANCIENT MAXIM OF HERMES proclaims, "As above, so below." Jesus also said, in a similar vein, "On earth as it is in heaven" (Matt. 6:10). So, why is this principle relevant? Because it attributes a nonphysical source (above, heaven) to material things (below, earth). Life for a materialist consists of what is perceived by the senses. Life for the spiritual aspirant consists of the mystical inner world, which may be far more real than anything perceived externally. The nonphysical sources are more subtle and causal in nature than their corresponding physical expressions. We'll apply this principle when examining physical and spiritual healing.

And so, any physical manifestation is said to have its nonphysical counterpart. This applies to all areas of life. In terms of illness and physical ailments, though very real and often very painful, these states of ill health have a corresponding nonphysical aspect which sometimes also includes a psychosomatic component. We often see how stress can cause ulcers, or prolonged distress can trigger either weight loss or weight gain. These are instances when the physical body and the nonphysical mind interact with each other and produce tangible expressions on the physical plane.

If a river is dammed, a stagnant body of water is often created. When the dam is removed, free flowing water clears out the stagnancy. Similarly, if there is congestion in the body, blockages are created and energy flow is stifled. According to Traditional Chinese Medicine (TCM), this is a recipe for illness. TCM and other healing modalities attempt to identify, then free these inner blockages so the *chi* or life force can flow freely without obstruction. This in turn creates an optimal environment for physical health.

Further, during deep states of meditation, experienced practitioners can immerse themselves in an inner reservoir of chi—or *prana* as it's known in Hinduism—which helps to recharge and revitalize their subtle, or energy body.

On a spiritual level, there are many inner psychological and emotional blockages that obstruct our perception of our soul or spiritual self, which is the gateway that allows us to perceive God. In Hinduism, these blockages are called *granthis* or knots. These knots must be untangled before we can gaze on our soul, on God, without impediments or obscurations. This process can be emotionally painful, as many memories and hidden behavioral patterns are often stirred up when they become dislodged during the disentangling process. However, this purgation is necessary. Once these entanglements are removed, the soul is liberated from their influence and can be experienced in its unencumbered luminosity, as can God.

From a spiritual perspective, true healing originates from the soul, from God, and funnels down through the physical body. The ultimate cure for the dilemma of life is to release our soul from all blockages and reside in the radiant, infinite Presence of God at all times. This is also the ultimate healing.

Brave, Truthful, and Unselfish
Website post: November 29, 2022

A NEW FILM VERSION WAS RELEASED this year based on the classic children's novel *The Adventures of Pinocchio,* about a wooden puppet that is brought to life and dreams of becoming a real boy. The story provides a wealth of fodder for spiritual metaphor, especially when Pinocchio is told he must be "brave, truthful, and unselfish" in order to transform himself into flesh and blood.

Metaphorically, the wooden puppet is the spiritual aspirant. Becoming a real boy—let's say a real person—is becoming spiritually enlightened. Three qualities are needed to bring about this metamorphosis, which we'll examine.

Bravery. A perfect example of bravery is the celebrated warrior Arjuna in the Hindu scripture, the Bhagavad Gita. Arjuna is overtaken by a paralyzing anxiety when confronted with the prospect of battling his own kin. "My body is trembling; I am feverish all over," Arjuna confesses (Gita 1:29–30). Then, in a moment of high drama, he throws down his bow (Gita 1:47) and declares, "I will not fight!" (Gita 2:9). But

113

the *avatar* Krishna rebukes him, saying, "Rid yourself of this petty weakness" (Gita 2:3). Upon admitting he is confused (Gita 2:7), Arjuna asks Krishna for advice. Krishna smiles (Gita 2:10), then imparts the great teachings of the Gita to his receptive student. This has the effect of reminding Arjuna who he truly is—his spiritual self, not his body, which is merely going through its karmic motions. Arjuna went on to fight and win the war, allegorically the daily battle of life we all undergo. Pinocchio, too, had to muster up bravery in order to emerge victorious after his many harrowing ordeals. The lessons for us: Be brave, and courageously and confidently seek enlightenment. And face all the vicissitudes of life with a calm, unperturbed mind.

Truthfulness. The Sufi mystic al-Junayd (830–910) said, "The essence of truthfulness means that you tell the truth in situations in which only a lie would save you."[69] Truth is simply conveying events as they actually occur without glossing them over. Yet, there seems to be a popular trend nowadays of telling lies. For Pinocchio, and especially for a spiritual aspirant, telling the truth is a *sine qua non* that can never be compromised. When Pinocchio lied, his nose grew, which readily exposed his lying. A spiritual aspirant's inner ledger—their conscience—similarly becomes stained through the act of lying. Being truthful also means being true to one's innermost spiritual nature, that is, following one's spirituality to the best of one's ability and diligently working to unfold it.

Unselfishness. Christians and Mahayana Buddhists both stress the importance of selflessness. "Love one another" (John 13:34) and "Work ceaselessly for the welfare and liberation of all beings" are the clarion calls of these two great religions. We are enjoined to expand beyond our self-centered boundaries by feeling compassion and expressing kindness toward others. Pinocchio demonstrated selflessness, as well as bravery, when he saved his human "father" Geppetto from certain death in the belly of the whale Monstro. With practice, we can cultivate an attitude of unselfishness within us. For a spiritual aspirant, selflessness should be their second nature.

In the end, Pinocchio became the real boy he wanted to be. The price of admission was his bravery, truthfulness, and unselfishness. We, too, as spiritual aspirants, can exponentially boost our progress toward enlightenment if we embody these same noble qualities.

Inner and Outer Transformation

Originally published in *Parabola* magazine
Volume 48, No. 1, "Transformation," Spring 2023

Be transformed by the renewal of your mind.[70]

–Paul of Tarsus

EVERYTHING IN THE UNIVERSE is predicated on change. As Heraclitus observed, "All things are in motion and nothing at rest." It may take millions of years for the clockwork to turn in the greater cosmos, but our lives change on a daily basis. In all aspects of life, we can substantiate the Buddha's assertion that everything is impermanent.

At any given moment, we are able to observe a snapshot of this change—in our day-to-day lives, in the world at large. We do not appear exactly the same as we did a decade ago. In many ways, the global state of affairs is different today from when the millennium began. But it's how we interpret these events that matters most. While there are common points of agreement, there are many common points of disagreement as well. All may decide to call a tall granite peak a "mountain," but how we perceive the mountain is another matter. To some, it is merely a feature in the landscape. To hikers, it serves as a challenge to be climbed. To miners, it is a source of minerals to be mined. While to dairy farmers, it provides pastures where they may graze cows for their livelihood.

And so, our perceptions differ. The way we perceive and interpret the outside world is a direct reflection of our inner state. Our perceptions, in turn, are dependent on many factors: our innate temperament; our family upbringing; the influences of our environment; and the conditioning we receive at home, at school, and from the vaster culture. Ultimately, however, we perceive things according to our level of spiritual evolution.

Traditional Vedic philosophy posits three primary ways that we perceive objects: (1) from a dualistic perspective; (2) from a qualified nondualistic perspective; and (3) from a wholly nondualistic perspective. This threefold division, contingent on our subjective, spiritual point of view, is based on the ageless axiom, "as within, so without."

On an intellectual level, we can readily grasp these differences. Our mind and cognitive faculties are hardwired for duality. Our dualistic self routinely interacts with a dualistic world. But strip away one layer of this apparition, and we are granted a glimpse of what is termed qualified nondualism. The world is both real and unreal. It is not yet an illusion, as is perceived in a fully nondual state, but rather it is *illusory*. Alice has one foot in this world, while her other foot is firmly planted on the far side of the Looking Glass.

Then, peel back the final sheath of the invisible coating that separates us from the ultimate reality. Down the rabbit hole we plunge, and there is no turning back. The innermost core of our being—our spiritual self—directly perceives the innermost core of the substratal reality. We begin to oscillate at the same frequency as the mysterious sacred. In this sublime state, we are connected with an unbounded ocean of interconnectedness that stretches beyond infinity. No matter what our actions are, our spiritual essence is conjoined with the underlying nondual reality that we recognize both inside and around us. The Katha Upanishad declares of this exalted state, "Though one is sitting, their spiritual Self travels afar; though lying down, it moves everywhere."[71]

However, when immersed in the world, we often undergo a tug-of-war between our spiritual and secular selves. The challenge for us is how to maintain a connection with the nondual core of our being while interacting with a seemingly all too real dualistic world. If we reside in a cave and sustain ourselves on nothing but *chi*, we can live, move, and have our being in nonduality uninterruptedly. But when groggily waking up in the early morning, getting equally sleepy kids off to school, commuting our labyrinthine 35-minute drive to work, engaging with sometimes moody coworkers, and battling a temperamental computer all day, it's a different matter.

The familiar Bookmark prayer of St. Teresa of Ávila begins, "Let nothing disturb you." And so, when riding the choppy waves of duality, we must ask ourselves: How would St. Teresa react when shamelessly cut off in traffic? If we are forced to lay off an employee, in what manner would Dr. Martin Luther King, Jr. deliver the unwelcome news? Exactly how might Lao Tzu cope with a serious illness?

This is where training comes in. We may soar with the angels during our meditation session, but how do we ground the experience afterward? Both states can coexist; this has been demonstrated by numerous accomplished mystics from all spiritual traditions. It's a matter of developing new habits by teaching our minds to maintain the same state of realization continuously. But this is far easier said than done.

St. Francis de Sales, the amiable French Catholic saint, is best known for his classic treatise, *Introduction to the Devout Life* (1609). The Bishop of Belley, who was Francis' friend and disciple, wrote of him, "Every year he paid me a week's visit, and before he came I took care to have some holes pierced in the doors or boarding of his rooms, that I might closely observe his behaviour when quite alone. Well, I can truly say that whatever he did, whether he prayed, read, meditated, or wrote, in his lying down and in his rising up, at all times and in all circumstances, he was the same—calm, unaffected, simple—his outward demeanour corresponding with the interior beauty of his soul. Francis quite alone was the very same as Francis in company."[72]

We, too, can integrate the spiritual and secular aspects of our lives so there is no division. Accomplishing this inner integration indeed takes training, but in so doing we are consciously evolving ourselves. Philosopher Gerald Heard provides a time-tested roadmap for the spiritual wayfarer: "There is a purpose, however obscure, in evolution [which is] to evolve consciously, to evolve consciousness. ... That evolution is now achieved and achieved only by the skilled, conscious training of our spirits."[73] Thus, we are called upon to intentionally accelerate our own spiritual evolution so that we, too, can walk in the footsteps of St. Francis de Sales. As we might envision St. Teresa, Dr. Martin Luther King, Jr., or Lao Tzu calmly navigating the sometimes rocky road of life, we can similarly train ourselves not to react to the seeming disturbances in the world. We can learn to retain the same inner poise and express boundless compassion under all circumstances when interacting with others. We can strive to remain calm amid life's adversities.

Over time, our spiritual training will yield tangible results in the various spheres of our lives. The key factor is commitment, which Tibetan Buddhists call *samaya*. The great Nyingma lama Patrul Rinpoche likened one's efforts to maintain samaya at all times to that of keeping a mirror spotless during a sandstorm. It must continually be cleansed. Similarly, it is important for us to renew our commitment on an ongoing basis if we are to succeed. If we are highly motivated to unfold the state of enlightenment within ourselves, our effort is never a tiresome chore. It becomes part and parcel of our character—a guiding principle that we joyfully incorporate and implement throughout life.

When such single-minded devotion to our goal becomes second nature, obstacles within us that might otherwise prevent our further spiritual development are more readily overcome. Negative emotions and unproductive habit patterns loosen their grip and are less likely to hold sway over our behavior. Love, generosity, and selflessness supplant any propensities to the contrary. Malice and ill-will flee from us quicker than the Devil from the Mount of Temptation. We come to embody the noble ideals we espouse; there is no longer any division between the two. The once-dominant kerfuffle of duality that raged within us becomes silenced and recedes into a faint memory. Ultimately, we come to perceive no distinction between our innermost spiritual selves and the spiritual essence of others. All superficial differences are eradicated in our all-consuming vision of unity.

Further, our spiritual illumination spills over and radiates into the world around us. We come to view the world anew, with illumined eyes. Our life becomes a beacon of calmness and compassion, which spreads as if by osmosis, touching those with whom we come into contact. One lone candle kindles the inspiration for others to likewise change. As this grows, an even greater conflagration of selfless love and universal peace proliferates. As Mahatma Gandhi insightfully reflected, "If we could change ourselves, the tendencies in the world would also change."[74] Our inner transformation produces outer transformation. Darkness gives way to light. At that wondrous stage, all apparent barriers are broken. Where there is no division, all is one.

The Holy Baptism

Excerpt from website post: January 9, 2022

"When Elizabeth heard Mary's greeting, the baby leapt in her womb ..." (Luke 1:41). Even before his birth, John the Baptist recognized she who would bear Jesus, as his spiritual connection with Jesus was so unusually, supernally strong. The holy players were assembling, and the heavenly portal was about to open.

On that blessed day of Jesus' baptism, John sensed the presence of Jesus even before he laid eyes on him. He stood in awe when Jesus appeared. John knew this marked the moment in time when God's spiritual blessings would be imparted through him to Jesus, acting as a key that would unlock—and unleash—the power of the Holy Spirit.

Jesus approached John, and they immediately recognized one another. John humbly acknowledged Jesus as the "one who is more powerful than I" (Mark 1:7). Then Jesus stood in the Jordan River, and John anointed him with the baptismal waters. In that sacred pouring of the holy waters, the spiritual power of God within John, raging strong from years of ascetic practices, was transmitted to Jesus. Immediately thereupon, the spirit of God—the Holy Spirit—entered Jesus. At the conclusion of their holy rendezvous, John had fulfilled his principal mission in life: "He must increase, and I must decrease" (John 3:30).

The transmissions which occurred on that exalted day opened the divine gateway. As the heavens rumbled, the unlimited power of the Holy Spirit was released and descended refulgent, infusing Jesus. "This is my beloved Son, with whom I am well pleased!" (Matt. 3:17).

Jesus' sacred initiation originated directly from God, as mediated by John, and from that point on Jesus came into his full powers. The Holy Spirit was now activated and became active within him. Jesus then withdrew into the wilderness to consolidate the omnipotent Holy Spirit energy within his being and bring forth its full manifestation. As a result, he was able to baptize others "with the Holy Spirit and with fire" (Matt. 3:11). Jesus rooted himself so firmly in his Heavenly Father that nothing could deter his vision or disturb his realization. Thereafter, he was ready to begin his mission.[75]

Cultivating Enthusiasm in Spiritual Life

Website post: September 11, 2023

WHEN FIRST EMBARKING ON THE SPIRITUAL PATH, many aspirants are filled with exuberance as they undertake their newfound pursuit. And no wonder—it's often like opening a door into an entirely new world. Unquestionably, spiritual aspirants should dive into their practices with wholehearted passion when seeking to unfold the deeper spiritual truths within themselves and radiating these inner treasures into the world.

But what happens after a year or five years or twenty years on the path? Are we as enthusiastic as in our younger days? After the initial honeymoon period of spiritual practice is over, daily spiritual life can settle into a routine, if not a rut, for those who survive this initial phase. We go through the motions, but much of the joy and associated ebullient feelings have long since faded away.

So, how can we maintain our fervor as if we were beginners? How do we infuse our spiritual practice with ongoing ardor?

The answer can be found in how we maintain our joy and drive and passion throughout many of life's routines and events. We somehow learn to renew within ourselves our *joie de vivre*, which buoys our family life, our career, and our mundane routines as we live our daily lives. We avoid settling into a rut, and we don't give up when adversities strike.

But what of our spiritual practices? Are we still deeply in love with God? Has our meditation routine stagnated? Do we mechanically go through the motions without really tasting joy in our practice? The Hindus have a word for taste—*rasa*—which in this context means palpably feeling the effects of our practice. These "fruit of the spirit" (Gal. 5:22–23)—love, joy, peace, patience, kindness, goodness, faithfulness, gentleness, and self-control, according to St. Paul—collectively interweave within us to become a living, experiential reality that scintillatingly embraces the very core of our being.

Our challenge is to overcome any jadedness we feel in our spiritual routines. For this, we can adopt the enthusiasm of a novice practitioner. This means fostering a "beginner's mind," as Sōtō Zen Master Shunryu Suzuki enjoins. In this way, we cultivate a youthful mindset—one of wonder and curiosity, lightheartedness, and ardent faith. As Jesus counsels, "Unless you change and become like little children, you will never enter the kingdom of heaven" (Matt. 18:3).

To carry on the status quo will not suffice if we are to make real progress. Our practice cannot be mechanical; it needs to be fueled by passionate longing. We must jettison our adult frame of mind during our spiritual routines and, with an attitude of innocence and openness, we are able to continuously renew our inner joy when walking our path. We can thereby inject passion into our practices, which fuels our spiritual journey. Cultivating enthusiasm in our spiritual life on a daily basis will make all the difference.

Did They Really Say These Things?
Website post: August 26, 2022

WE HAVE AT TIMES READ seemingly unbelievable statements from the saints. We will briefly analyze three such sayings.

Hasidism is a well-known spiritual movement within Judaism. Rabbi Yisrael Friedman of Ruzhin (1796–1850), honored as a great *tsaddik*, a revered Hasidic holy man, is said to have called miracles "child's play." Huh? On the surface, this is an incredible assertion. However, upon digging deeper, we read in a fascinating account[76] that Rabbi Friedman viewed miracles as secondary to the "upper worlds," which are the more spiritual ones, and that "wiser" holy men go beyond the realm of miracles to these higher worlds. Elsewhere,[77] we read that the rabbi thought of miracles as distractions that detract from more purely spiritual ends. And so, the lesson gleaned from the rabbi's terse, instructive words, is for spiritual aspirants not to spend time dabbling in psychic phenomena, such as reading minds or developing the ability to perform miracles, but rather to focus exclusively on God in their spiritual strivings.

St. Catherine of Genoa (1447–1510), a standout among Catholic mystics, said, "I see without eyes, I understand without understanding, I feel without feeling, and I taste without taste."[78] What in the world? On the surface, this baffling statement appears to defy logic. However, when we look below the surface, we are able to find some clues. When a mystic enters into deep spiritual communion, their sense of self is dissolved. It's hard to fathom, but their inner spiritual essence merges with the universal spiritual Essence that is God. In such a state, a mystic may sometimes experience a kind of omniscience. Our interpretation of St. Catherine's sublime words is that she indeed underwent a deep mystical experience, whereby her sense of self was so attenuated that she identified with the omniscient omnipresence of God.

In Orthodox Christianity, we read of advanced spiritual adepts, called *starets* (Russian) or *geron* (Greek). A preeminent Russian Orthodox monk, St. Seraphim of Sarov (1759–1833), is considered one such *starets*. The following quote is attributed to him: "Acquire a peaceful spirit, and thousands around you will be saved."[79] Hmmm … how can this be? For our answer, we will consult a decidedly non-Christian text, the Yogasūtra of Patanjali. A rough translation of aphorism 3:24 states, "By focusing exclusively on the qualities of kindness, compassion, and the like, one develops these same qualities." In a Christian context, we would suggest that St. Seraphim so thoroughly focused on putting into practice Jesus' counsel to "love one another" (John 13:34) that he became, as it were, love incarnate. It is written of him that wild animals would peacefully gather around his meditation hut. His aura of unconditional love radiated far and wide, and many who came within his orbit were deeply affected by the love he tangibly emanated. Hence, he could make such a statement based on his own personal experience.

These three saints, as with many saints, live in "upper worlds" that we can only imagine. But they leave us signposts, sometimes using paradoxical, enigmatic, and even irrational language, to convey their elevated spiritual experiences, which lie beyond the rational mind. Yes, they did indeed say these things, using words that refer to even more wonderful things that can never fully be conveyed in words.

Vedanta in a Nutshell
Website post: September 9, 2022

VEDANTA IS ONE OF THE SIX traditional schools of Hindu philosophy. The word *Vedanta* means the "end" or "conclusion" of the Vedas. However, I will interpret *Vedanta* as the "culmination" of the Vedas. The Vedas are ancient, revealed hymns wherein Hindu religion originated. They contain writings known as the Upanishads, which hold the kernels of Vedanta philosophy. *Veda* means "knowledge." The implication is that the culmination of all knowledge is contained in the Vedanta philosophy. And so, what is the culmination of all knowledge? The knowledge of God, the ultimate reality.

Because of differing philosophical interpretations, there are three main branches of Vedanta: dualism, qualified nondualism, and pure nondualism. Shankara (ca. eighth century A.D.) is considered the key proponent of nondualism. However, we still have not said what Vedanta is in real-life terms.

In a nutshell, Vedanta is the realization of one's innermost nature, one's spiritual self, which is called the *atman* in Vedic thought.

The atman is said to be one with Brahman, the universal, ultimate reality. Hence, one of the "Great Sayings" (*mahavakyas*) in the Upanishads is *Tat Tvam Asi*, meaning "you are That"; that is, your innermost spiritual essence is the same as the ultimate reality. Another Great Saying is *Aham Brahmāsmi*, which means, "I am Brahman"; that is, our real "I"—our spiritual self, not our superficial ego—is identical with the ultimate reality.

All this is fairly heady stuff. So, on a practical level, how does one realize these truths? By diligently practicing one of the yogas, or paths to Union with God. There are four principal yogas that are geared toward one's temperament—*bhakti* (for devotional-oriented aspirants), *jnana* (for intellectual-oriented aspirants), *karma* (for activity-oriented aspirants), and *raja* (for meditation-oriented aspirants)—as well as many minor ones. However, a person can combine all four yogas into one grand synthesis by applying them in all aspects of one's life. (By the way, hatha yoga postures are a subset of raja yoga, and are not in and of themselves considered a pathway to God.)

Okay, so let's get to the nuts and bolts of Vedanta. Through dedicated spiritual practice, a person can transform themselves so they experience nonduality. This is not the same as merely intellectually adopting a nondual philosophical viewpoint, but rather experientially realizing in our innermost essence that "we live and move and have our being" (Acts 17:28) in God, in Brahman—the ultimate reality. This is the core of Vedanta.

A third Great Saying from the Upanishads is *So'ham*: "I am He." No, this does not mean that your ego is one with God—far from it. In God there is no ego, no differentiation. All separation is gone, all dividing lines eradicated. Enlightened saints relate that they experience a vast ocean of oneness—forever blissful and filled with infinite peace—and their innermost nature is part of this oneness, even as their mind and body go through the motions of their daily lives. This is Vedanta in a nutshell. We, too, can experience this searing realization, which is the culmination of all knowledge.

The Perils of Teaching Spirituality
Website post (extract): September 24, 2023

ONE OF THE TOPMOST PERILS when walking the spiritual path is if one feels called to teach spirituality to others. I'm not referring to credentialed religious ministers who are sanctioned by their church or religious order, or to scholars who impart knowledge about religion in a classroom setting. In the context of Christianity, St. Paul readily acknowledges that certain individuals take on such spiritual roles as a result of an innate vocational calling, which is biblically authorized. Paul expressly condones such activities: "And he gave some as apostles, some as prophets, some as evangelists, some as pastors and teachers ..." (Eph. 4:11).

I am referring to the self-styled, often self-appointed "authority" figures—the so-called spiritual teachers, gurus, and the like—who characteristically present themselves as enlightened, or who at least position themselves as experts who are more knowledgeable about spirituality than you or me. But their actual authority may be questionable, and underneath the surface may lurk a massive ego. They consider themselves adepts, and we their potential disciples. Yet the image they project may be a complete illusion, and many are in it only for the money. (For more information, visit my webpage "Spiritual Teachers,"[80] which discusses this topic at length.)

Jesus taught that the foremost requirement of a spiritual teacher is humility: "Whoever among you would be first must become the servant of all" (Mark 10:44). Jesus himself washed the feet of his disciples (John 13:5)—one of the most awe-inspiring acts of humility in recorded history, in my opinion.

The Hindu mystic Sri Ramakrishna repeatedly warned against "spiritual teachers" who are either jumping the gun or are acting on their own initiative without divine sanction. They may in fact be no more spiritually advanced than the rest of us. "Everybody is anxious to be [a] master. How many are there who would care to be disciples?"[81] He continues, "It is a difficult task to teach others. One can become a true spiritual teacher only when one has realized God and received a Divine commission from Him. ... For the teaching of Divine truths a badge of authority is indispensable. A man who tries to teach others without it will be laughed at. He cannot get realization himself and he tries to show the way to others. It is like the blind leading the blind. In this way more harm is done than good."[82]

Spirituality cannot be taught like a classroom topic. Learning facts about spirituality or memorizing dogma is not true spirituality. Spirituality is assimilated in one of two ways: (1) it can be *transmitted*, and even then, by a capable, competent teacher (but this merely lays the groundwork, because the student must practice in order to integrate the imparted spiritual energy within their being); and (2) it can be experientially realized by a diligent practitioner who has a keen desire to follow and attain the fruits of the path they follow.

In a recent teaching, the Dalai Lama stated, in essence, that if he were "sitting on a high throne and telling lies," he could not be trusted, and thus his actions must accord with his speech.[83] And therein lies the crux of the matter. Ideally, a teacher is authenticated by a legitimate tradition, and any genuine teacher *does* practice what they preach, and they practice spiritual disciplines as well. And, ideally, such a teacher possesses a degree of heightened realization. Otherwise they merely spout empty, flowery words and often lead others astray by their dubious claims of inner realization and at-times hypocritical lifestyle.

Along these lines, Christian minister John MacArthur wrote a blistering, no-holds barred, *Emperor's New Clothes* assessment about Christian televangelists.[84] However, we see spiritual frauds sprout up in religious traditions and spiritual organizations other than Christianity, so buyer beware.

The issue of deceptive spiritual teachers and misleading teachings has long interested me. Decades ago, I made charts that detailed the misinformation promulgated by a number of bogus spiritual teachers of the day, and I even specified many such teachers. But yesterday's cadre of questionable teachers has been replaced by an equally objectionable welter of scam artists and con persons who pollute the current spiritual scene. There is nothing new under the sun. Many well-respected and popular "spiritual" teachers do not impress this observer in the slightest, while their audiences sit with jaws agape and purchase their slickly promoted products by the cartful. This is symptomatic of the watered-down pablum that can readily be sold to the gullible masses by using shrewd marketing techniques. This blatant commercialism from blatantly commercial, so-called spiritual teachers litters the spiritual landscape, as does the plethora of noxious "self-help" entrepreneurs, who typically offer little or nothing related to genuine spiritual transformation.

Imparting spiritual teachings involves, basically, *becoming* the teaching and transmitting the teaching from that level. This occurs during bona fide initiations and empowerments. Ideally, the teacher transmits the core elements from their religious tradition that will lead an aspirant straight on the road toward enlightenment. Thus, it is critical to revisit the teachings of St. Paul, Jesus, Ramakrishna, and the Dalai Lama on this topic. Ramakrishna said that the word "guru" was one of the "words which prick me to the core ... God is our only spiritual guide."[85] Let us remember his wise words.

And so, these are some of the many essential caveats and cautionary admonitions about the very real perils of teaching spirituality. Once again, caveat emptor.

Lao Tzu and the Tao

Excerpt from lecture delivered at the Friends of the Spirit
study group in Redding, California: March 19, 1987

Perhaps the best way to understand the philosophy of the Tao Te Ching—"The Classic Treatise on the Way and its Essential Characteristics"—is just to read it, without the embellishments of extensive interpretation or commentary. The manuscript's purported author, Lao Tzu, who is said to have lived during the sixth century B.C., sets forth his ideas, though not without paradox and ambiguity. Still, his work is sometimes misinterpreted, often leaving the impression that he advocated quietism, nihilism, or moral relativism. However, nothing could be further from the truth, and such allegations can readily be discounted.

Throughout the course of the book's 81 chapters—consisting of some 5,250 characters—Lao Tzu's philosophy is revealed to be highly ethical, highly practical, and accountable both to the spiritual and material realms of life. He doesn't condone licentiousness or a wanton lifestyle. He looks not to the obvious but to the underlying cause. He does not advocate the shuffling and rearranging of society; instead, he teaches the inner transformation of the individual, which, in turn, brings about societal change.

Taoism has no personal God; rather, Lao Tzu believed in a universal principle—the ultimate reality—which he called the Tao, "The Way." By living in harmony with the Tao, one assimilates its essential characteristics, its "Te." A person can then approach life with an entirely different perspective. They see that things happen of their own accord, and that situations are not to be forced. They are readily adaptable to changing circumstances rather than being rigidly stubborn and inflexible. They work without seeking recognition instead of hankering after fame or looking for approval from others. They opt for the uncomplicated rather than the elaborate. They neither exploit nor harm others. By following the Tao, a person attains unruffled peace of mind. One becomes childlike and innocent, yet ancient and wise at the same time. When this occurs, that person is considered an accomplished knower of the Tao.

Carrying One's Cross
Website post: April 9, 2022

Whoever would be my disciple must renounce themselves and take up their cross and follow me.

–Matthew 16:24

THESE MEMORABLE WORDS OF JESUS clearly set out the conditions by which one may become his close disciple in Jesus' physical absence. We'll analyze the deeper meaning of his statement.

My disciple. Jesus indicates that a person can have an intimate, lasting spiritual relationship with him. This requires an ongoing commitment, through good times and bad, come what may.

Renounce themselves. We are so full of ourselves that we have no idea how refreshing it might be if we could shed ourselves for a while. Not only to the benefit of ourselves, but perhaps for those around us as well. Jesus places no time limit on how long we must renounce. We will presume he meant for the duration of our life.

This means reducing our swollen egos and tempering our often bull-in-a-China-shop personalities to more apportioned degrees.

Give up the primacy of self and adopt a humbler posture in daily life. The mystic can go even further and lose their self entirely in the infinitude of God during focused spiritual practices. In Sufism, the intractable ego is called one's *nafs* (technically, the *nafs al-ammareh* [Koran 12:53], "the passionate, egoistic soul"[86]). Virtually all Sufi practices are intended to subdue one's *nafs* in order to fully attune oneself to God. Less self equals more God. And so, as Jesus proclaimed, "Blessed are the poor in spirit, for theirs is the kingdom of heaven" (Matt. 5:3).

Take up their cross. This is the hard part. It's easy to practice spirituality when everything goes our way. But what about when the storms of life arrive? It's precisely how we endure the tumultuous situations in life that tests our spirituality. If our commitment is superficial, we'll buckle under. But if our faith is solid, we'll pass through the storms undaunted.

Follow me. In his one-sentence injunction from Matthew 16:24, Jesus has given us three preconditions to be met before we can, in his words, "follow me": (1) make a long-term commitment to be his disciple; (2) renounce our ego's stubborn, self-centered proclivities; and (3) gracefully handle all the burdens of this life. Once these preconditions are met, then we can "follow me." Are we ready?

Where All Roads Lead
to Greater Love
Website post: November 27, 2023

WE KNOW ALL TOO WELL from reading the daily headlines that there's plenty of negative news to go around. There are six or so current wars; there have been around 600 mass shootings in the United States to date this year alone, which is dumbfounding and should shock us to the core; and there is an alarming grassroots movement in this country to topple democracy as we know it in favor of autocratic rule. These are just the tips of the iceberg.

But a recent period in the United States was also beset by a bloody, prolonged war; mass civil unrest; and horrific political assassinations—the 1960s. However, unlike our present times, the spirit of the Sixties held out the promise of three things that are conspicuously absent from today's world—universal *love*; *hope* in a better future for all; and *idealism* that sought a peaceful, even utopian existence for humankind and planet earth.

In December, two major religious observances are celebrated that are grounded in hope: the Jewish Festival of Lights, known as Hanukkah, which celebrates a miraculous occurrence, and which inspires Jews to this day; and the Christian birth of Jesus, which similarly celebrates a miraculous event, and which has brought hope to millions of people for two millennia. Thankfully, we still hear the message of universal love and the ideal of peace for all humankind being preached in various religions. Yet, much of institutional religion has lost its unifying influence, and people argue over petty denominational differences. And all too frequently, and most sadly, we witness religious wars, where many are killed in the name of God, which is utterly reprehensible.

Moreover, the current social climate is more divisive and splintered than ever. There is no single guiding principle that can unite the many wrangling, fractious social groups, often composed of self-serving special-interest cliques. Where can love and peace be found amid these quarreling factions?

Stepping back from all this, I recall several songs from the 1960s that actually contained Jesus' words "Love one another" (John 13:34): "For Pete's Sake," "Get Together," "People Got to Be Free," and "Sweet Cherry Wine." ("He Ain't Heavy, He's My Brother" comes very close.) If needed, you can google these songs to identify the associated musical groups and lyrics to jog your memory. There are also Jackie DeShannon's two anthems: "What the World Needs Now is Love" and "Put a Little Love in Your Heart." And of course the Beatles' "All You Need is Love." Love, peace, hope, and similar idealistic principles were a staple of the radio airwaves back then, extending into the early 1970s. Where can similar idealistic-based popular songs be heard nowadays?

Reminiscing like this isn't just some schmaltzy, bead-wearing, flowers-in-your-hair, patchouli-scented, retro-throwback to the Summer of Love, or a wistful wish to live in Pleasantville. Rather, I'm noting a marked contrast between the undercurrent of universal love, hope, peace, and idealism that fueled much of the Sixties, and that of today's world in which such ideals are sorely lacking.

Some may argue that the free-spirited, liberal approach of the Sixties is responsible for many of today's woes. But an argument could be made against this as well, as conservative forces then and now have cast their own long, often ugly shadow. There were violent oppositions on both sides of the political spectrum back then as well as now. Such upheavals always seem to occur whenever oppressed groups struggle for greater rights (e.g., the Civil Rights movement) or, mind-bogglingly, when people protest against war and want a peaceful world (e.g., the Kent State shootings). Or, as in the case of India's independence, sociopolitical mayhem can occur when peaceful people nonviolently struggle for their right to freedom, absurd as this may seem. I'm simply pointing out that we need bridge-building and unifying principles to forge a society of trust, mutual respect, and hospitable relationships. And so, "Love one another" can serve as a guiding principle. Or, at the very least, people can act with civility and courtesy toward one another by practicing the Golden Rule.

The roads in our society now diverge in all directions that are strewn with an abundance of hateful signage. But a roundabout can be constructed that unites them all. This roundabout must be paved with goodwill, compassion, and tolerance. When this occurs, we will travel down a convergent highway where all roads lead to greater love.

Diwali – Festival of Lights
Excerpt from website post: December 9, 2021

Today marks a major religious festival celebrated by Hindus, Sikhs, and Jains around the world. Known as Diwali, or the Festival of Lights, devotees decorate temples, their homes, streets, and public places with lamps and lighted candles. The festival symbolizes light overcoming darkness and the triumph of good over evil.

Any contemporary mystical aspirant can also participate in Diwali by symbolically kindling the flame of spirituality within their heart. God is omnipresent and dwells within each of us. We can find and experience God there. By stoking the light of God inside ourselves, we are figuratively celebrating the victory of spirituality over worldliness. That divine light blazes brightly, so much so that all darkness is doused, all negativity extinguished.

Like the phoenix rising from the ashes, the mystical message of the Festival of Lights is for us to triumphantly rise above our worldly limitations and establish our inner connection with God. Diwali is celebrated both outwardly and inwardly on this joyous day. From within us, the flame of God's infinite light, love, and peace extends outward to all quadrants of the universe, touching all beings and transforming the entire creation. One tiny light grows to illumine the entire cosmos.

Emotional Stability
and the Spiritual Life

Originally published in the May–June 1981 issue,
No. 179, of *Vedanta for East and West*

OUR PURPOSE IN SPIRITUAL LIFE is to undertake the process of consciously accelerating our own spiritual evolution. In order to do this, we must, as a first step, make concentrated efforts to rid ourselves of those physical and psychological drives that stand in our way. The great Indian saint Sri Ramakrishna (1836–1886) tells us that once we earnestly begin our struggle to realize God, grace will descend to loosen the bonds that tie us to *maya* (i.e., dualistic limitations). "The more you move towards the light," he said, "the farther you will be from darkness." Our job is simultaneously to remove the obstacles (*avidya maya*) that prevent our innate God consciousness from unfolding and to cultivate those aids (*vidya maya*) that help it to emerge.

This implies that we employ in our spiritual strivings what philosopher Gerald Heard (1889–1971) called "athleticism"—a "skilled persistence" that will enable us to control those desires and attachments which distract us at every turn. To see a distant object through a telescope, one must line it up in the lens and then focus in sharply. Likewise, we must sharply focus all of our energies to attain our one goal: the acceleration of our own spiritual evolution. "The average man has numerous desires," says Swami Swahananda,[87] "but the spiritual seeker has one resolute thought—spiritual illumination. The secret of his success is concentration."

When we are not concentrated on attaining our goal, we are, therefore, distracted. As it is maya's "duty" to keep us unconscious, many such distractions may not readily be apparent to us. Thus, as spiritual aspirants it will benefit us to pause and examine some of the various obstacles that divert our attention from God.

The life of a human being can be seen to consist of five major aspects: (1) extraphysical (outside the body); (2) physical (the body); (3) emotional; (4) mental; and (5) spiritual. These five facets of our lives can also be categorized according to the degree of their subtlety, as the Vedic Sankhya philosophy maintains, in which event we can reverse this order. As all life has a spiritual basis, the mental, emotional, physical, and extraphysical aspects of life would be categorized in these respective positions—from the finest to the grossest. Our first task, then, is to decide what level of priority we assign to each of these different areas of our lives. We will assume that the most subtle, the spiritual, should receive the highest priority, while the least subtle, the extraphysical, should receive the lowest.

Our gauges for determining this level of priority might be several criteria of discrimination that we can adopt and use to discover what role any particular person, thing, habit pattern, or value plays in our spiritual lives. Thus, we might ask ourselves, "Does this particular person, attitude, or thing aid or hinder my search for God? Will it lead me to God; does it remind me of God? If not, why do I cling to it? What do I *really* want?"

By doing this, we may find that many of the priorities we have heretofore valued in our lives can now be seen as excess baggage no longer needed or desired on our journey to God. As such, they can easily be dispensed with and replaced by a new, thinned-out set of values. Further, as we rearrange our priorities in this manner, we not only simplify our lives but also narrow our range of interests and are thereby able to focus more and more of our attention on our spiritual goals. Next, we will examine how this assessment and rearrangement of priorities might best be accomplished.

The extraphysical sphere of life involves our friends, the type of work we do, and all those outside interests and activities that constitute the environment in which we live. If we apply the criteria of discrimination to this area of our lives, we may find, for example, that it is necessary to cultivate new friends, friends who pursue spiritual goals similar to our own. The atmosphere at work and in the home should be calm and conducive to quieting the mind. We may also ask, "Which of the hobbies and amusements I currently enjoy are in accordance with my spiritual pursuits?"

Looking to the physical or bodily aspect of our lives, we can easily reason that, as Swami Shivananda[88] says, "For spiritual advancement one must first make the body strong." The body is the vehicle in which we realize God, and we can best care for it by exercising it regularly and giving it pure and easily digested food. At the same time, we should avoid giving it those things that we know are harmful, such as tobacco, alcohol, non-medicinal drugs, and junk food.

When we apply the criteria of discrimination to the mental facet of our lives, we can readily determine what is and what is not essential in our search for God. The saints tell us that it *is* essential that the mind be trained not to lose itself in the myriad of desires which bombard it. Rather, it must be gently and persistently reminded of its primary purpose in life—to break free from its bondage. When it wanders, we must catch it. When it wanders again, we must catch it again, telling it the same thing over and over again. If we persevere in this practice, the mind, in the end, will cooperate.

But what about our all too unruly emotions? Emotion originates from our various attachments and aversions. It is the force that puts life into our actions and decisions. It is the vitality that injects *feeling* into what we do and think. Occasionally, this free-flowing vitality becomes bottled up. It should be allowed to express itself without repression but with the direction that spiritual discipline brings.

Emotion should not violate reason, nor should reason render our feelings impotent. Referring to Ramakrishna, Swami Shivananda tells us that his teaching is *"bhakti* [spiritual emotion] tempered with *jnana* [spiritual understanding]." This requires an interplay between our emotions and our intellect, both of which Ramakrishna said should be evenly developed in spiritual life. The secret is to avoid the extreme of emphasizing one at the expense of the other.

But how do we approach the problem of applying the criteria of discrimination to our emotions, which are often the most troublesome areas of our lives? We can safely start by examining one of the basic situations in a person's life—their aloneness, out of which spring many emotional devices the mind can use to postpone union with God. So, how does the approach of a spiritual aspirant differ from a worldly person's approach in coping with their aloneness?

We all grow up in a society that aims at maintaining order by making us conform to various rules. We—and this applies to spiritual aspirants in particular—are told by society that there is a "normal" way to act and react, and that we should never deviate from the standards that have been set for us to follow. If we do, we are often considered odd and branded as outcasts.

While this conformity helps maintain a basic cohesion to what might otherwise be an anarchic society, it all too often becomes a stereotyped standard to which we adhere, driven by the fear of what others might think if we acted on our own. In such instances, the society is strengthened at the expense of the individual. The individual is then taught to depend, emotionally, on what the crowd does rather than to rely on themselves, on their spiritual companions, and ultimately on God for all of the support and encouragement they need.

However, few people bother to give up those actions and habit patterns that cause them to seek emotional security in an unquestioning conformity to the social status quo. Yet Swami Brahmananda[89] advises, "Be self-reliant." We must sometime realize that as wayfarers on the spiritual path we *are* different from others, that we are "strangers in a strange land," as Robert Heinlein wrote. At some point, we must free ourselves from the notion that we share a commonality of experience with *all* people. No. We see through different eyes. Our expectations, goals, and experiences are different from those of others with a predominately secular bent. Ours are related to God; theirs are related to the world. As Ramakrishna says,

"The spiritually minded belong to a caste of their own, beyond all social conventions." We on the spiritual path have broken away from the ordinary worldly mentality in order to seek God. Therefore, we must be independent and free to pursue our spiritual goals, unaffected by the opinions and influence of others.

But this is where the trouble comes in. Having been raised to conform, we must now face the possibility of splitting off from the crowd, a prospect that might seem unbearable. We are accustomed to constant background noise and an endless series of calculated diversions that we hope will provide meaning to our lives, and we are loath to give these up in order to pursue a God of whom we're not yet sure. Unwilling to leave our lives of apparent security and comfort, we retreat from facing what seems to be a stark and lonely alternative. We have neither made a break from our emotional dependence on maya nor are we able to continue in our old ways. We are left holding a tiger by the tail. We are stuck.

And so by avoiding this, the ultimate and most important decision of our lives, we simply perpetuate the dilemma in which we find ourselves. If we really wish to be free, we must begin by accepting the fact that in choosing the spiritual life we have become strangers in this world. Otherwise, we'll end up making a compromise with life and try to adjust to it by conforming to the status quo, all the while privately despairing because of the spiritual choice we *didn't* make.

This is not to suggest that we are to cut ourselves off from the world in a kind of spiritual snobbery. Perhaps the Lord will bless us with the company of a few likeminded spiritual companions or bring us to a community of likeminded souls where a spirit of camaraderie and support can give strength and encouragement to our spiritual practices.

Sri Ramakrishna was fond of saying that a person could not see God as long as they were fettered by shame, hatred, and fear. Here he indicated not only the need for emotional stability in an age before psychology became a popular science, but he also linked the achievement of this stability directly to the spiritual path by implying that once totally freed from such emotional fetters, a person will see God. Therefore, we may conclude that the achievement of some degree of emotional stability is one of the first significant marks of progress in our spiritual life.

Now, what are some of the attitudes we can develop that will free us from many of the emotional dependencies that could easily be classified as obstacles to our spiritual evolution? For one thing, it would no doubt help if we attempted at all times to understand our intentions and motives in life and decide whether or not they are suited to our spiritual ideals. We should encourage those that are suitable, while we should abandon those that are not.

Second, we want to strengthen those aspects of our character that increase our desire both to realize God and to be free from all of the influences which neither lead us to nor remind us of God. We need to have controlled minds and be in control of our own lives, neither dominating nor being dominated by others. Having a sense of personal independence and a firm confidence in our spiritual convictions helps make us fearless and frees us from anxieties and apprehensions about the future.

"Real strength knows how to bend and yet regain its true position." Here Swami Turiyananda[90] speaks of the need for us to be firm in our principles yet flexible in the particulars of life, readily adaptable to changing circumstances without losing our spiritual bearings. Ramakrishna also asks us to "be devotees and not fools." So, and third, while practicing the virtue of forbearance with all people, we must also be realistic and know that certain people will take advantage of us. As Ramakrishna counsels, we must be prepared to "hiss" without malice if such an occasion arises, and to "salute from a distance" all those who would interfere with our attempts to realize God.

There is a saying, "The price of freedom is eternal vigilance." If we can develop an ongoing interest in working on ourselves at all times, we shall be, as Ramakrishna teaches, "hoisting our sails" to catch the breeze of God's unconditional Grace that is always blowing. If we can gain an unshakable intellectual certainty that emotional stability is an essential part of our spiritual growth, then we can effectively do battle with the sloth that would otherwise prevent us from doing our part to perfect ourselves.

Furthermore, we must *confront* our negative emotions, not adjust to them. Only then can we conquer them. Only then will we be more ready to emerge from the cocoon that maya has woven around us and to prepare ourselves to live a balanced spiritual life, firm in our convictions, fearing no one, and certain of ourselves and of our Supreme Goal.

Summary:
- Our purpose in spiritual life is to remove the obstacles that prevent our innate God consciousness from unfolding and to cultivate those aids that help it to emerge.
- We must sharply focus all of our energies to attain our one goal: the acceleration of our own spiritual evolution.
- Ask yourself, "Does this particular person, attitude, or thing aid or hinder my search for God? Will it lead me to God; does it remind me of God? If not, why do I cling to it? What do I *really* want?" By so doing, we may find that many of the priorities we have valued in our lives can now be seen as excess baggage no longer needed or desired on our journey to God.
- The achievement of some degree of emotional stability is one of the first significant marks of progress in the spiritual life. We must develop an ongoing interest in working on ourselves at all times in order to reach our spiritual goal.

[Ed. note: This article, originally appearing in the May–June 1981 issue of the U.K.-based Ramakrishna Vedanta Centre's magazine *Vedanta for East and West*, addresses an audience that is familiar with the Ramakrishna–Vedanta tradition. In 2006, Swami Dayatmananda served as Minister of the Ramakrishna Vedanta Centre. We are grateful to Swami Dayatmananda for his kind assistance in 2006 in facilitating the (eventual) republication of this article.]

Three Questions

Excerpt from website post: February 24, 2024

The most effective way a person can know if God exists is to have a direct personal experience of God. This is best accomplished through spiritual practices. God no longer remains an objective concept or an abstract entity but rather a living presence that palpably touches and envelopes our soul on the deepest level. Spiritual practices such as prayer, devotion, contemplation, and selfless service unquestionably aid us in our quest to personally encounter God. But the overriding ingredient that will exponentially propel our spiritual journey is a keen desire to know God. When this deep yearning wells up inside us, we will be drawn to God like iron filings to a magnet. Eventually, what began as our concept about God transforms into a vivid, unmistakable, tangible experience of God.

And so, we must ask ourselves: What is my spiritual goal? Ideally, nothing short of full-blown spiritual illumination. We must also ask ourselves: Will any given activity in my life lead me to or away from my spiritual goal? Such frank self-examination helps us clearly discern our path and clear out the obstacles and distractions that stand between us and our spiritual goal.

Now, if we live in the world, we must compromise to a degree. If we throw out the baby with the bathwater, we might end up unemployed, homeless, penniless, and friendless. Hmmm ... come to think of it, this is exactly what happened to St. Francis when he decided he would *not* compromise one iota.

Time is ticking, and we can renew our commitment on a daily basis so we prioritize our spiritual goal above all other goals each moment in our lives, without hesitation or excuses.

The Most Important Lesson
Previously unpublished parable: April 2022

ONE MORNING IN HEAVEN, the young angels Philip and Clare leisurely strolled through the Golden Fields. The day was young, and there was much joy to be had. Hand in hand, they ventured near the Gates. Suddenly, Philip stopped and gazed ahead. He grew perplexed at what he saw. Clare gently smiled, for she was wiser than Philip and knew of his innocence.

Philip asked, "What is the purpose of the Dividing Line? Many souls pass over this line and enter our Gates. But many good souls are turned away at the Dividing Line; they are escorted to the Abode of Lesser Resplendence, just below our sacred realm, even though they performed virtuous deeds and engaged in constant devotions."

Clare consoled him, for they were angelmates, and they encouraged one another and delighted in each other's company. "This is for the Mentor to answer. The ones who are turned away had not learned the most important lesson."

Philip asked, "How can I learn of this lesson?"

Clare said, "Go to the Mentor. He will show you." Upon uttering these words, a great concern filled Clare, for she knew what would come to pass. She had always hoped Philip would be spared the vision of the Nine Sorrows. But her hope dwindled on that fateful day.

Approaching the Mentor, Philip explained his puzzlement. The Mentor listened carefully, then replied, "Your wings will be withdrawn. You will now be shown what you must learn."

In an instant, before he and Clare could say their goodbyes, Philip was sent to Earth, where he appeared in human form, twenty-five years of age, with soft features, befitting his gentle angelic disposition. But he could not be seen by mortals; he was invisible to them. As Philip's wings had been withdrawn, and as an angel's powers are forever linked to their wings, Philip was prevented from performing good works.

And every day while on Earth, Philip was mystically brought to one of nine different places, where a different scene unfolded.

One day he was shown famine. The soil was parched. There were no crops, as the land was barren and could not produce harvest. And the famine-stricken wept, for there was great sadness. Philip stood, and he silently witnessed, but lacking his magical wings, he could not intervene, which caused him much grief.

Another day he was shown war. There was destruction and hatred, and carnage and death. And the war-torn wept, for there was great sadness. Philip stood, and he silently witnessed, but lacking his magical wings, he could not intervene, which caused him much grief.

Philip was then shown hunger. There was wailing, and the wasting away of children, and much suffering for want of food. And the hungry wept, for there was great sadness. Philip stood, and he silently witnessed, but lacking his magical wings, he could not intervene, which caused him much grief.

Another day he was shown a broken family. There was much unhappiness and discord. The children couldn't understand, and they suffered amidst their parents' many fights. And the children wept, for there was great sadness. Philip stood, and he silently witnessed, but lacking his magical wings, he could not intervene, which caused him much grief.

Then Philip was shown poverty. There was barely enough food to eat, barely enough clothing to wear. Those who lacked food starved, and those who lacked clothing shivered. And the poor wept, for there was great sadness. Philip stood, and he silently witnessed, but lacking his magical wings, he could not intervene, which caused him much grief.

Philip was then shown homelessness. There was no shelter for countless multitudes, and many destitute families huddled together at night. The displaced were scorned and vilified. And the homeless wept, for there was great sadness. Philip stood, and he silently witnessed, but lacking his magical wings, he could not intervene, which caused him much grief.

Another day Philip was shown bigotry. There was much ill will and fear, and name-calling and reviling. Philip, with his angel eyes of pure love, saw that all people were the same inside. But others saw only outer differences. And the victims of bigotry wept, for there was great sadness. Philip stood, and he silently witnessed, but lacking his magical wings, he could not intervene, which caused him much grief.

Then Philip was shown disease. There was much suffering and pain. Waves of sorrow spread among the afflicted, the stricken, and the disabled. And the ill and sickly wept, for there was great sadness. Philip stood, and he silently witnessed, but lacking his magical wings, he could not intervene, which caused him much grief.

Then lastly, Philip was shown ignorance. Many could not afford an education; others were simple and of limited intelligence. But all were shunned and regarded as fools, and they were loathed. And the so-called ignorant wept, for there was great sadness. Philip stood, and he silently witnessed, but lacking his magical wings, he could not intervene, which caused him much grief.

And every day, Philip was shown these things. Each day he was led to a different place on a different continent. And the days accumulated. And lo, before long, a hundred years had come to pass, for Earth has no want of famine and war and hunger, and broken families, and poverty and homelessness, and bigotry, and disease, and ignorance.

But one hundred years for an angel passes like a gentle breeze over the land. And so, the Mentor returned Philip back to Heaven.

Clare, who had kept vigil from afar, rushed to greet her beloved angelmate. They joyfully embraced one another, then headed toward the abode of the Mentor. The two angels appeared before him, where they stood together holding hands. But Philip looked sad, for his heart had been scarred by his many visions of the Nine Sorrows.

And the Mentor said, "Philip, tell me what you have learned."

Philip spoke, "I have witnessed many things. I now know why many good souls are turned away at the Gates. Indeed, they have not learned the most important lesson. They may be good and they may do good, but they lack the one thing that will gain them Heaven."

The Mentor asked, "And tell me, what is that one thing?"

Philip replied, "Love. The one thing they lack is love."

The Mentor smiled, "You have learned well, my son. You have come to understand the importance of love. It is by expressing wholehearted love for one another and unconditional selflessness toward one another that mortals may be granted the keys to Heaven. Behold, your wings are now restored."

The Mentor continued, "I will send you back to Earth for another hundred years. And you will revisit those same places. And you will witness those same scenes. But this time, you will be able to intervene, and your grief will turn to joy. You will use your angelic powers to bring love to every scene you witness. With love, you will heal the hopeless. With love, you will mend the wounded. With love, you will bridge many gulfs. And with love, you will sow lasting seeds that sprout and thrive. Go now, and bring love to this crushed planet in order to restore its broken spirit."

Clare's heart leapt inside her, for she was filled with boundless joy upon hearing of Philip's mission. Then Philip went about his task. He appeared invisibly on each continent. And every day, through the mystical powers conferred on him by his magical wings, he spread love across the Earth. As the Mentor had predicted, his grief turned into great rejoicing.

And lo, people began working together. Nations cooperated with one another in harmony. They brought food to the hungry, clothing to the destitute, and shelter to the homeless. They reconciled their petty differences, and peace flourished everywhere. A dark veil was lifted from the realm of mortals. People's hearts were opened, and they saw with new eyes. They began to value love over money, altruism over self-interest, and the greater good of the planet and all its inhabitants—from animals and sea creatures and birds, to forests and oceans and grasslands, to humans of all ages from every walk of life—above all other concerns.

And the Earth began to heal.

At the end of the hundred years, Philip once again returned to Heaven. He and Clare embraced each other in great delight. One morning, they leisurely strolled through the Golden Fields. The day was young, and there was much joy to be had. Hand in hand, they ventured near the Gates. Then Philip stopped and gazed ahead. A smile appeared on his face. Clare, too, gently smiled, for she was wiser than Philip and knew what he had learned.

Philip exclaimed, "It's gone! There is no longer a Dividing Line. All souls from Earth now pass directly through the place where the line once stood and enter our Gates. For they have learned the most important lesson. And that lesson is love."

All You Need Is Love
Excerpt from website post: February 14, 2022

The unambiguous title of the Beatles' huge 1967 Summer Of Love hit says it all. Not only does this song stand the test of time, but the group's modern-day anthem about love also stands the test of eternity. Why? Because love truly is all we need, both individually and collectively.

Both Christians and Tibetan Buddhists especially focus on developing universal, limitless love toward all living things. The Tibetans as well as other Mahayana Buddhists refer to this unlimited altruism as *bodhichitta*. Christians double up on love, following Jesus' counsel both to love God and to love one another, which in turn is based on the sublime Jewish teachings in Deuteronomy 6:5 and Leviticus 19:18.

However, something happens to those who truly espouse this teaching. The more one falls in love with God, the more universal does one's expression of love become. Like a small pond overflowing with water after a drenching rain, one's love increasingly grows in magnitude until it cannot be contained. It overflows everywhere. Love then entirely overtakes a person and they become a living embodiment of infinite love. Spiritual love, divine love, selfless human love, universal love: all such distinctions melt away as a torrent of radiant, unlimited love emanates unceasingly from their being. God is seen in all beings, and all beings in God. Everything is perceived as a boundless ocean of pure limitless love.

And so, what is needed, not only on this St. Valentine's Day, but always? All you need is love.

Notes

[1] Tao Te Ching, Chapter 1.

[2] Rabindranath Tagore (trans.), *Songs of Kabir* (New York: Macmillan, 1915), p. 91.

[3] Gerald Heard, *The Code of Christ* (Eugene: Wipf and Stock, 2007 edition), p. 123.

[4] Paul Reps (compiler), *Zen Flesh, Zen Bones: A Collection of Zen and Pre-Zen Writings* (Rutland: Tuttle, 1958), p. 19.

[5] Tao Te Ching, Chapter 16.

[6] Plotinus, *Enneads*, VI, 9:11.

[7] Psalm 46:10, *Common Bible: The Revised Standard Version of The Bible* (New York: Collins, 1973).

[8] Adapted from *Sermon XXIII, On the Feast of St Matthew, Apostle and Evangelist* (1498), by Johannes Tauler.

[9] William D. Conner, *The Fiction of Time* (1959), http://www.iwaynet.net/~wdc/timefic.htm, accessed Jun. 2009.

[10] William D. Conner, *New Analysis of Time* (1999), http://www.iwaynet.net/~wdc/time.htm, accessed Jun. 2009.

[11] Charles T. Tart, *States of Consciousness* (New York: E. P. Dutton, 1975), p. 125.

[12] Chandogya Upanishad, II.23.3.

[13] Rabbi David Cooper, "God is a Verb" (Berkeley, California: live lecture at Black Oak Books, Sept. 23, 1997).

[14] Tart, op. cit., p. 125.

[15] Paul Davies, *Other Worlds* (New York: Touchstone/Simon & Schuster, 1982), p. 42.

[16] Swami Swahananda (trans.), *The Chandogya Upanishad* (Madras: Sri Ramakrishna Math, 1956), pp. 417–418.

[17] Gerald Heard, *Pain, Sex and Time: A New Outlook on Evolution and the Future of Man* (New York: Harper & Brothers Publishers, 1939) p. 301.

[18] Gerald Heard, *Training for the Life of the Spirit,* (Eugene: Wipf and Stock, 2007 edition), pp. 61–62.

[19] Jan van Ruysbroeck, as cited in *The Adornment of Spiritual Marriage*, in Dom C. A. Wynschenk (trans.) and Evelyn Underhill (ed.), *John of Ruysbroeck* (London: J. M. Dent & Sons, 1916), p. 152.

[20] Ibid., pp. 152–3.

[21] Ibid., p. 149.

[22] *Are 'nones' hostile toward religion?*, https://www.pewresearch.org/religion/2024/01/24/are-nones-hostile-toward-religion/, accessed Mar. 2024.

[23] *Vatican Sets Record Straight on Sexual Abuse*, https://www.catholiceducation.org/en/controversy/common-misconceptions/vatican-sets-record-straight-on-sexual-abuse.html, accessed Mar. 2024.

[24] *Child Sex Abusers in Protestant Christian Churches: An Offender Typology*, https://www.qualitativecriminology.com/pub/osa148h6/release/2, accessed Mar. 2024; and *Data Shed Light on Child Sexual Abuse by Protestant Clergy*, https://www.nytimes.com/2007/06/16/us/16protestant.html, accessed Mar. 2024.

[25] *The sexual abuse scandal rocking the Southern Baptist Convention, explained*, https://www.vox.com/culture/23131530/southern-baptist-convention-sexual-abuse-scandal-guidepost, accessed Mar. 2024.

[26] *Is there more sexual abuse in the Protestant Churches than the Catholic Church?*, https://stopabusecampaign.org/2018/01/08/is-there-more-sexual-abuse-in-the-protestant-churches-than-the-catholic-church/, accessed Mar. 2024.

[27] Gerald Heard, *Training for the Life of the Spirit*, (Eugene: Wipf and Stock, 2007 edition), p. 13.

[28] Alan Watts, *Man in Nature* (New York: Mystic Fire Video, 1993, originally taped in 1971).

[29] Ibid.

[30] Gerald Heard, *The Creed of Christ* (Eugene: Wipf and Stock, 2008 edition), p. 90.

[31] Ibid., pp. 64–65.

[32] *Selections from Swami Vivekananda* (Calcutta: Advaita Ashrama, 1975 edition), p. 131.

[33] Swami Tapasyananda (trans.), *Srimad Bhagavadgita* (Mylapore: Sri Ramakrishna Math, 1984), p. 61.

[34] *Teachings of Sri Ramakrishna* (Calcutta: Advaita Ashrama, 1971 edition), p. 269.

[35] His Holiness the Dalai Lama, *Avalokiteshvara Initiation* (Leh, Ladakh: live webcast, Jul. 23, 2023).

[36] Mahendra Nath Gupta, *Sri Sri Ramakrishna Kathamrita*, Vol. 1, Sect. 1, Ch. 6, Mar. 5, 1882 (Chandigarh: Sri Ma Trust, 2024), online

edition: https://www.kathamrita.org/kathamrita/volume-1-section-1, accessed Mar. 2024.

[37] *Shohei Ohtani Is My Favorite Athlete, But Paying Him $700 Million Is Bonkers,* https://nymag.com/intelligencer/2023/12/shohei-ohtani-is-the-best-but-paying-him-usd700m-is-bonkers.html, accessed Dec. 2023.

[38] *Shohei Ohtani, Lionel Messi, Patrick Mahomes and Biggest Contracts in Sports History,* https://bleacherreport.com/articles/10099129-shohei-ohtani-lionel-messi-patrick-mahomes-and-biggest-contracts-in-sports-history, accessed Dec. 2023.

[39] Adapted from (1) *The Sacred Books of the East, Vol. XV, The Upanishads,* Friedrich Max Müller (trans.), *The Mundaka Upanishad,* Third Mundaka, First Khanda, Verse One, (Oxford: Clarendon Press, 1884), p. 38; and (2) *Eight Upanishads, Volume Two,* Swami Gambhirananda (trans.), *The Mundaka Upanishad,* Third Mundaka, Canto I, Verse One, (Kolkata: Advaita Ashrama, 1958), p. 116 ("of divergent tastes").

[40] Paul Jackson, S. J. (trans.), *The Hundred Letters,* by Sharafuddin Maneri (New York: Paulist Press, 1980), pp. 35–36.

[41] Brother Lawrence of the Resurrection, as cited in *The Practice of the Presence of God,* "Second Conversation" (New York: Fleming H. Revell Company, 1895), p. 11.

[42] Ibid., p. 20.

[43] Henry David Thoreau, *Walden; or, Life in the Woods* (1854), "Economy."

[44] Ibid., "Where I Lived, and What I Lived For."

[45] Ibid., "Economy."

[46] His Holiness the Dalai Lama, *Teachings for Tibetan Youth, Day 2: Manjushri Blessing* (Dharmsala, H.P.: live webcast, May 31, 2023).

[47] All New Testament citations in this essay (except for 1 Cor. 13:12, which is the author's own composite rendition) are acknowledged as follows: Scriptures taken from the Holy Bible, New International Version®, NIV®. Copyright © 1973, 1978, 1984, 2011 by Biblica, Inc.™ Used by permission of Zondervan. All rights reserved worldwide. www.zondervan.com. The "NIV" and "New International Version" are trademarks registered in the United States Patent and Trademark Office by Biblica, Inc.™

[48] *Visible Light,* https://science.nasa.gov/ems/09_visiblelight, accessed Apr. 2023.

[49] *Visible Light: Eye-opening research at NNSA,* https://www.energy.gov/nnsa/articles/visible-light-eye-opening-research-nnsa, accessed Apr. 2023.

[50] Gerald Heard, *The Five Ages of Humanity* (Nevada City: Sky Parlor Publications, 2023 edition), p. 215.

[51] This is the author's composite rendition of St. Teresa of Ávila's Bookmark prayer, which was discovered in her breviary after her passing.

[52] This is the commonly rendered version of St. Francis de Sales' saying.

[53] John Roger Barrie, *Dialogues With the Lord of Time* (Nevada City: Sky Parlor Publications, 2023), p. 107.

[54] Ibid.

[55] The author is grateful to Elizabeth Krajewski, Ph.D., for her valuable comments on the text.

[56] Adapted from *The Mending of Life* (ca. 1340), chapter 11, by Richard Rolle.

[57] Adapted from (1) *Teachings of Sri Ramakrishna* (Calcutta: Advaita Ashrama, 1934 edition), p. 28; and (2) *Gospel of Sri Ramakrishna (According to M., a son of the Lord and disciple),* Vol. II (Madras: Sri Ramakrishna Math, 1928 edition), p. 32.

[58] Judith M. Tyberg, Ph.D., *The Language of the Gods* (Los Angeles: East-West Cultural Centre, Second Edition, 1976), p. 37.

[59] In May 2021, it was reported that NASA's Voyager 1 space probe detected a faint but steady background hum in interstellar space, vibrating at frequencies between approx. 3.0 and 3.1 kilohertz. However, at that frequency range, the sound is more like a bosun's whistle than a hum. From a spiritual perspective, one might conclude that the universe whistles a jolly little tune as it continually brings itself into existence and stretches itself throughout the farthest reaches of space and time.

[60] Another method for achieving *nadi-shuddhi* is *pranayama,* typically interpreted to mean breathing exercises. Yet, *pranayama* actually translates as "regulating the *prana.*" Prana is the vital energy that animates the body and mind; it is synonymous with *chi* in Traditional Chinese Medicine. Prana circulates through the *nadis,* but usually flows in an irregular manner because of various blockages. When prana is intentionally regulated, it then circulates more efficiently and uniformly

throughout the organism, thus cleansing the nadis by clearing out these blockages. However, regulation of the prana spontaneously occurs during the higher stages of contemplation and devotion as a *byproduct* of these attainments. By achieving nadi-shuddhi through these more subtle and ultimately more effective means, the practice of breathing exercises becomes unnecessary.

[61] Adapted from (1) *The Condensed Gospel of Sri Ramakrishna* (Mylapore: Sri Ramakrishna Math, 1911), pp. 176–177; and (2) Swami Abhedananda (ed.) *The Gospel of Râmakrishna* (New York: The Vedanta Society, 1907), pp. 243–244.

[62] H. A. Reinhold (ed.), *The Soul Afire: Revelations of the Mystics* (New York: Pantheon Books, 1944), p. 293.

[63] Raymond Van Over (ed.), *Eastern Mysticism, Volume One: The Near East and India* (New York: New American Library, 1977), p. 382.

[64] Ralph Waldo Emerson, "Self-Reliance" (1841).

[65] "Q&A: Diana Ross," *Rolling Stone* magazine, Nov. 13, 1997, online edition: https://www.rollingstone.com/music/music-news/qa-diana-ross-230900/, accessed Mar. 2024.

[66] *Punishingly brutal report is devastating for Boris Johnson*, https://www.bbc.com/news/uk-politics-65913299, accessed Mar. 2024.

[67] *Atman of Hindus and Anatman of Buddhism*, https://www.youtube.com/watch?v=A13Q57thkgI, accessed Oct. 2022.

[68] His Holiness the Dalai Lama, *Commentary on Valid Cognition – Chapter 2* (Dharmsala, H.P.: live webcast, Oct. 4, 2022).

[69] Barbara R. Von Schlegell (trans.), *Principles of Sufism*, by Al-Qushayri (Berkeley: Mizan Press, 1990), p. 193.

[70] Romans 12:2.

[71] Katha Upanishad 1.2.21.

[72] Jean-Pierre Camus de Pont-Carré (the then Bishop of Belley), *The Spirit of St Francis de Sales*, trans. by J. S., (London: Burns Oates & Washbourne, 1925), pp. 286–287.

[73] Gerald Heard, *Training for the Life of the Spirit*, (Eugene: Wipf and Stock, 2007 edition), pp. 12–14.

[74] Mohandas K. Gandhi, "Accidents: Snake-Bite," *Indian Opinion*, Aug. 9, 1913.

[75] Concluding benediction by the author: "And so, we pray this day that the Holy Baptism of Jesus may inspire and renew our own souls;

that the sacred waters of God's grace may fill us with the Spirit of God; and that the transformative power of the Holy Spirit may descend into our very being and actuate the living, palpable presence of God."

[76] *Hasidism: Writings on Devotion, Community, and Life in the Modern World* (Waltham: Brandeis, 2020), pp. 105–106.

[77] "Wonder of miracles," *The Jerusalem Post*, Nov. 8, 2012, https://www.jpost.com/jewish-world/judaism/wonder-of-miracles, accessed Sept. 2022.

[78] Baron Friedrich von Hügel, *The Mystical Element of Religion as Studied in Saint Catherine of Genoa and Her Friends* (London: Dent, 1909), p. 276.

[79] "'Acquire a peaceful spirit,' said St Seraphim" – Google Search, Aug. 2022; and *St. Seraphim of Sarov*, https://orthochristian.com/72651.html, accessed Mar. 2024.

[80] *Spiritual Teachers*, https://www.johnrogerbarrie.com/spiritual-teachers/, accessed Sept. 2023.

[81] *The Gospel of Sri Ramakrishna* (San Francisco: San Francisco Vedanta Society, 1912), p. 113.

[82] *The Gospel of Ramakrishna* (New York: The Vedanta Society, 1907), pp. 167–169.

[83] His Holiness the Dalai Lama, *Teachings for Tibetan Youth, Day 2: Manjushri Blessing* (Dharmsala, H.P.: live webcast, May 31, 2023).

[84] *A Colossal Fraud*, https://www.gty.org/library/blog/B091207, accessed Sept. 2023.

[85] *The Gospel of Sri Ramakrishna* (San Francisco: San Francisco Vedanta Society, 1912), p. 113.

[86] Titus Burckhardt, *An Introduction to Sufi Doctrine*, trans. by D. M. Matheson (Lahore: Sh. Muhammad Ashraf, 1988), p. 151.

[87] From 1976 until his passing in 2012, Swami Swahananda served as Minister of the Vedanta Society of Southern California.

[88] Swami Shivananda (1854–1934) was a direct disciple of Sri Ramakrishna.

[89] Swami Brahmananda (1863–1922) was a direct disciple of Sri Ramakrishna.

[90] Swami Turiyananda (1863–1922) was a direct disciple of Sri Ramakrishna.

ABOUT THE AUTHOR

John Roger Barrie is the longtime literary executor of influential author, historian, lecturer, and philosopher Gerald Heard (1889–1971), and the creator and publisher of geraldheard.com, online since 2002. He has overseen reissues of eighteen classic Gerald Heard titles, both nonfiction and fiction. Previously, he served for many years as a regional freelance writer and editor.

For nearly five decades, Mr. Barrie has practiced spiritual disciplines from a variety of different religious traditions, and he has studied with and received blessings from numerous spiritual teachers. Raised a Catholic, he has intentionally followed the spiritual path since 1974, branching out thereafter to embrace an interfaith approach while maintaining his Christian roots.

Specifically, the traditions he has explored and teachers he has encountered include Theravada Buddhist monks from Burma and Sri Lanka; Japanese and Korean Soto and Rinzai Zen masters; lamas from all four Tibetan Buddhist schools, including H. H. the XIV Dalai Lama, as well as several "first generation" lamas hailing from Tibet prior to the diaspora; Cistercian and Trappist Catholic monastics, including Fr. Thomas Keating and Fr. Basil Pennington; he also attended a dozen or so services of different Christian denominations to learn about them firsthand. The list of traditions and teachers further consists of Hindu monks, including several "second generation" swamis from the Ramakrishna Order; Vishnu Tirth lineage monks; and teachers from additional Hindu centers. He studied with Hasidic and Renewal rabbis, including Rabbi

Schneur Zalman Stern and Rabbi Avram Davis; shaykhs from three different Sufi orders; a Chinese internal Chi Gung expert; and Taoist adepts. He explored Native American religion and studied with teachers versed in Native American traditions. He also became credentialed in two energy-healing modalities.

During 1986 and 1987, he founded and moderated Friends of the Spirit, a small, informal, nonacademic study group in comparative mysticism based in Northern California, for which he produced 19 original essays, many of which are scheduled to be published in future books. In the mid-1990s, he was privileged to undertake volunteer writing projects for several respected religious teachers, including Shaykh Taner Ansari, Father Thomas Keating, Rabbi Schneur Zalman Stern, and Swami Shivom Tirth.

His first published spiritual article appeared in the May 1981 issue of *Vedanta for East and West,* and he has since published occasional articles on Gerald Heard and spirituality, including four original contributions for *Parabola* magazine. His first book, the acclaimed spiritual novel *Dialogues With the Lord of Time,* was published in 2023. *The Deepest Silence and Other Essays on Contemporary Spirituality* is his second book. He continues to publish a running blog on his website, *Explorations in Contemporary Spirituality,* online since 2006, and he posts occasional videos on his YouTube channel, launched in 2023.

Mr. Barrie is honored to have a longstanding teaching authorization as a lay instructor in the Ramakrishna–Vedanta tradition from the late Swami Swahananda of the Ramakrishna Order.

Mr. Barrie's interfaith approach incorporates teachings and practices from many religions and spiritual paths, including the rich mystical traditions from his native Christianity, and the universal principles advanced by the respected, interfaith-oriented Ramakrishna–Vedanta tradition. His emphasis on experiential spiritual realization and his firsthand familiarity with diverse spiritual traditions has imbued him with a fluent knowledgebase and practical outlook when addressing the subtleties of the mystical path. For more information, visit johnrogerbarrie.com.

John Roger Barrie lives in Northern California with his wife.